Dogmanship

A Horseman's Ponderings

Tom Moates

Other Books by Tom Moates:

Discovering Natural Horsemanship
Round-Up: A Gathering of Equine Writings
Six Colts, Two Weeks, Volume I
Six Colts, Two Weeks, Volume II
Six Colts, Two Weeks, Volume III
Considering Horsemanship
Mane Thoughts
The Christian Horseman's Companion
The Old Sleeper, A Spy Novel

The Honest Horsemanship Series:
A Horse's Thought
Between the Reins
Further Along the Trail
Going Somewhere
Passing It On

Dogmanship

A Horseman's Ponderings

Tom Moates

ISBN 979-8-9918028-0-2
Cover design by Emily Kitching.
Front cover image by Carol Moates.
Rear cover image by Carol Moates

Contents

Introduction .... *i*

Chapter One — Titus 1

Chapter Two — The Signals We Send 13

Chapter Three — Conditioned Response vs. Willing Partnership 20

Chapter Four — Kona and Marcy 33

Chapter Five — Why Being Nice Alone Doesn't Always Work 43

Chapter Six — Titus Two 49

Chapter Seven — Gladys 53

Chapter Eight — School's Out 59

Chapter Nine — Calmness vs. Excitement 65

Chapter Ten — Straightness 73

Chapter Eleven — Observation 79

Chapter Twelve — Working with Ellie Mae 85

Chapter Thirteen — Leading 93

Chapter Fourteen — Nuances of Training 99

Chapter Fifteen — The Big Fork in the Road 105

Chapter Sixteen — So They're Started, So They Go 111

Chapter Seventeen — Discipline vs. Punishment 117

Chapter Eighteen — My Next Dog 123

End Note 131

About the Author 135

This book is dedicated to the dogs and horses of the world, who enhance the lives of people--may we return the favor.

Introduction

Horses and dogs.

In my world, these two creatures in particular hold special relationships to humans. An all-consuming desire to get better with horses catapulted me into the realm of horsemanship. Out of that obsession, more than a dozen horse books and hundreds of articles on horses have flowed. I've made some big strides working with horses, to the point that for years now teaching horsemanship clinics and lessons is as much a mainstay to my livelihood as is writing on the subject of getting better with horses.

But dogs. Dogs keep circling back to the forefront of my mind. Their potentials, challenges, and connections to humans keep my mind stirred up. And it's a curiosity to me that I was around dogs for a couple of decades before I went all loopy over equines, but I'm better versed in working with horses than with dogs. I learned a long time ago that getting better with horses is not always related to how much time a person has put in working with them. There's something else that needs to be at play that helps a person to get better with horses—an understanding of how they tick and how to establish a better relationship with them. I'm finding the same to be true when working with dogs.

In the past half decade or so, my wife Carol has volunteered to work with dog rescues. This also led to my volunteering to help her, and take on some tasks with the rescue dogs. This experience has provided me with access to a great number and variety of dogs that have a spectrum of personalities, positives, and problems. What an education!

The fascination with which I still pursue horsemanship steadily is bleeding over into my curiosity with dogmanship. My approach to horsemanship is unique in the horse world and is derived from my learning directly from horseman Harry Whitney over a couple of decades now. It is an approach to horses that seeks to develop relationships between horses and humans so that horses can find relaxation, okay-ness, and with-you-ness with their people. The main ingredient for the remarkable success of such an approach is getting the horse's mind centered up and available, and then directing horse thoughts to establish a willing partnership and seemingly weightless connection between the two species.

My successful work with horses seems to share common characteristics with my ongoing education and challenges of working with dogs. The experience to date clearly indicates to me that there are similarities and differences to getting things done and establishing good relationships with these two animals. For some time now, I have been exploring what works with dogs, discovering what doesn't, and I am truly fascinated with where horsemanship and dogmanship overlap, and where they do not.

Other than references to the dogs that Carol and I and our family members have owned, the dogs' names in this book have been changed to keep them anonymous. The points I make, the lessons I've learned, and the ideas I consider from interactions with a range of dogs, many of them rescues, are in no way diminished by concealing their true identities. My intention is to explain my own experiences, thoughts, and lessons accurately without putting anyone else, or the dogs they may have fostered or adopted, in the spotlight.

This is a book about my quest to get better with dogs, and how that looks as I come to the task by looking through the lens of some decent successes with horses. Writing this book, as with my many horsemanship books, is as much an exercise of me clarifying in my mind what I am learning to be true as it is a means of sharing what I am learning and thinking with others. I hope that the reader finds my experiences and lessons as helpful and entertaining and as I did in recording them onto the page.

Mirage and me on a ride with Miles, my neighbor Teddy Carter's miniature Poodle, along for the fun. (Photo: Teddy Carter)

Chapter One
Titus

One of the first formative dogmanship experiences that presented itself when working with rescue dogs came when I worked with a little sandy colored, wire-haired terror of a terrier named Titus. Maybe just a wee bit bigger than an artisan loaf of bread but, in apparently typical terrier fashion, the little booger fancied himself a giant. Titus's reputation with the dog rescue volunteers as being a handful seemed accurate when I entered the kennel room and met him for the first time.

The kennels ran in a long, single row along the left side of an aisle way as I entered. The interior dividers between kennels were solid sheet metal from the ground to about waist high. Above that was chain link fencing. A large hound and a bull dog mix were visible in the two kennels closest to me, but the others were blocked from view by the solid dividers. However, my attention was drawn about two-thirds of the way towards the far end where a little whitish head with scruffy ears popped up and then disappeared, popped up and disappeared, over and over again like a kid on a pogo stick behind a fence. A constant yapping accompanied the hairy head added, no doubt, for good measure.

"That'll be Titus," I thought.

A pretty strong negative, knee-jerk reaction to the little fella swelled in me from the outset as I witnessed his behavior. The yapping and bouncing only intensified as I approached his kennel for a closer look at the rascal.

Part of helping my wife Carol with her rescue dog duties at that time involved taking the dogs out to a run behind the building to do business and get out of the confines of the kennels for awhile. Getting a dog out meant opening a chain link kennel door and stepping or reaching in and placing a slip-lead (a leash with a slip-knotted loop at the business end) over a dog's head. Then leading the four-legged beast down the aisle way, passing through a door to a hallway, and then going through another door to the outside, fenced-in, graveled area. There was plenty of time in all of that for things to go well or not so well. I stayed quite curious as to what each new dog would present for challenges or positives during our first few times of going to the turnout together and back again.

Like I do when fetching a horse from a stall, I immediately begin to size-up the relationship between the dog and me from the moment I approach the confined critter. By this point, maybe a year into helping with kennel duties, a few items on my dogmanship list were fully formed. One of the big ones was that for any dog, including the unruly ones, I did not open the kennel door until the beast behind it displayed some calmness. At first, that could be a really tall order for dogs accustomed to obtaining freedom through the door by barking, getting wound up, and jumping on it.

Taking the time it takes to stand there waiting for a change in mindset as dogs do whatever pushy behaviors they are accustomed to doing can be very hard for people, me included. Waiting for a real change of mind requires time and patience, but it also requires the confidence that the dogs will begin to search out other options besides being boisterous if you wait them out. Eventually, though, dogs tend to try a variety of things to get the stupid human to understand that they want out.

Sometimes, I add a slap to my leg, stomp my foot, or say "Hey!" to try and help a wound-up dog get a change of thought—these are actions that I sometimes use to get a horse's mind centered up with me. Although these often do work with dogs, they do not seem to work as consistently well with dogs as they do with horses.

In this "conversation" with a dog at a kennel door, at some point, the list of what the dog tries usually includes settling down somewhat and sitting. Get consistent with not opening the door until the dog behind it is calmly sitting or lying down, and before long you may discover a dog who settles and readily relaxes when you arrive to let him or her out rather than a crazed, barking, jumping monster. Or, at least at first, get a dog who is able to calmly sit with a simple reminder of some kind. People reinforce the bad behavior when they allow it to work out for the dog and open the door when a dog is going nuts. In some pretty difficult cases that I've witnessed, people even tossed in treats for the dogs when they were aggressively on the kennel door to distract them across the kennel so the door could be opened—and food treating a dog for that behavior really can help solidify exactly what is not wanted. The opposite side of that coin is to be proactive and reinforce the desired behavior by having a plan to get calmness as the key to opening the door, and sticking to it.

As my horsemanship mentor Harry Whitney is fond of saying about horses, "It's amazing what they won't do if you don't

My horsemanship mentor Harry Whitney.

let them." That is applicable here, too. He doesn't mean that you absolutely force a horse to do or not do something, but rather that you make the unwanted things not work out so well, and the horse in turn chooses not to do them. I am finding that there is truth to this in the world of dogs, as well.

Standing at the door to Titus's kennel, it took the bouncing, barking terrier all of about 20 seconds to get the memo that I was sending. The scruffy rat intuited the idea to settle down so quickly that I blinked in amazement, wondering if what I was seeing was true? He searched for an answer to the kennel door problem right from the get-go with me, and that had an uplifting effect on my outlook for interacting with him. Titus's immediate turn-around, I think, was due to in part to the fast rate at which the little guy was able to go through a list of things that he might try to get what he wanted. Some dogs get the memo eventually but do not process the situation at the high rate of speed that Titus did.

This kind of quick thinking in a horse or dog isn't necessarily a sign of what we tend to think of as intelligence or creativity (an idea that I've come to understand after hearing Harry mention it when discussing horses at clinics). Rather, it is just processing speed. For example, an old computer might take 30 seconds to spit an answer out and a new top of the line computer does it in a nanosecond—the answers may be the same but the time it takes to get them may be vastly different. Is one computer "smarter" than the other? No, they form the same "thoughts." One just arrives at the correct answer more quickly. Titus had one of those very fast, new high tech processors, no doubt.

Still packing my preconceived notions about Titus's reputation and my own baggage about not particularly liking little, yappy dogs, I was not expecting to engage the critter much more than just getting things settled with him at the kennel door and quickly ushering him on-leash outside. As mentioned above, with horses, I am in the habit of making a fuss of some kind when their minds wander to get them mentally centered with me. Then, directing them can become a possibility. That kind of action with horses now is reflexive in me, and it just shows up when I am working with dogs. Once I cracked open the door to the kennel, Titus went to jumping again.

"Hey!" I exclaimed, slapping my thigh with my free hand instinctively as I would with a horse, and then I stood quietly and calmly. Titus said. "What? Yes?" and sat attentively in the floor looking up at me.

Then, opening the door was easy as he waited quietly, sitting with a curious look on his face about who this weirdo was, slapping his leg and insisting that he chill out before getting an opened door. I stepped partly into the kennel, on guard should he make a break for it, but he did not. He sat contentedly and waited as I placed the open loop of the slip lead over his head.

I don't know for sure what Titus was thinking, but I can tell you that I was intrigued at this point. The little terror with the reputation for being a snot was rather suddenly right there mentally with me, sitting and watching what I might ask of him next. There even existed a nice feel between us in that moment.

I retreated out of the kennel, and when I put a little touch on the leash for him to come, too, the little wiry-haired fellow shot out the door like a rocket and made a move to get out ahead of me. My equine sensitive reflexes kicked in again and instantly as he past my left leg I stomped my booted left foot on the concrete floor and put a bump on the leash. His attention was immediate and his gaze shot back at me questioningly. I put some feel on the leash and suggested that he take up a position behind me and follow my lead down the aisle way instead of being out in front of me. He fell in line with that arrangement after a few moments of struggling with the idea.

We walked together with that understanding between us maybe eight steps to reach the first door en route to the outside run. I stopped before the door. Titus stood to my left, a little prancy.

"Sit," I said.

Titus looked at me.

I looked at Titus.

Titus cocked his head a little, questioningly.

The expectation of getting through the door was palpable in him but I just waited. I had no idea if he knew what a verbal "sit" meant. Finally, he decided to try sitting. I reached down and petted him once on the head and then I reached for the door knob.

Somewhere along the line, and I am sure it came from more than one source although I don't remember specifically where, I discovered the idea that when a person is connected to a dog on leash, who goes through a door first (and, indeed, who is out in front of the other when traveling) is in the position of the leader in the dog's mind. And that order has consequences in how dogs perceive the position of the person relative to them and how they behave. And that sometimes can be a major deal and greatly define the relationship between the dog and the human.

If you are subordinate to the dog in the dog's eyes, then according the dog you'd better be listening and following him or her and not the other way around. And, thus they value the person's input far less than what we as humans would like. I learned long ago that some seemingly very small things with horses can have major impacts on the relationships with them, and thus influence how interactions unfold with them.

For example, it is not unusual to see, when asking a horse with the lead rope to step out and go around a person on a circle, the horse push into the person with a shoulder and the person back up. I take great care to be particular in that little spot and help others to be, as well, because that posturing has quite a significance to the horse. If the horse senses the person is yielding, then the horse can develop the habit of pushing on people. The horse can come to understand and expect that people get out of his way. The horse can follow up with thinking generally that if people yield to him physically, then it is the human's responsibility to follow what he presents.

This can become quite dangerous if a 1200 pound animal goes to pushing on people. That can get to the point of knocking a person down, stepping on a foot, and so forth. The relationship needs to be set up so that what the person offers is of consequence to the horse and that the horse becomes willing to let go of his thoughts and hear a person and be easily directed with a good and relaxed feeling about it. I think of these sometimes seemingly little particular things with horses a lot. And when I go to working with dogs, I carry along the assumption that there are similar particulars that are important to establish with canines. Who goes through the door first is one that caught my attention pretty early on.

With Titus now sitting at my left side, I took hold of the door handle, turned it, and began to swing the door open. The little rascal took that as his cue to bolt out in front of me through the door. Anticipating this, I was ready and he hit the end of the leash before getting through the door and I accented the moment with another loud stomp of my boot.

"No sir!" I exclaimed aloud.

I crowded the slightly opened door and Titus backed into the aisle way at a high rate of speed, eyes wide, and clearly aware that this situation was going to be different from how things usually went. I thought again of Harry's quote about horses, "It's

My wife Carol's dog Zeke on the left and my dog Ellie Mae on the right. Zeke was a Giant Schnauzer/Bullmastiff mix and Ellie Mae was part Belgian Malinois part German Shepherd. Here they had romped around and then found a big mud puddle on a hot day.

amazing what they won't do if you don't let them." This situation was my version of not letting him lead in our relationship. This was me explaining in no uncertain terms that him racing ahead of me through a doorway was not going to work out well. In no way did I punish him. I just made one of those well timed ruckuses right at the instant when the unwanted behavior was taking place that I use with horses, and it was enough to get the point across to the sensitive terrier.

The main reason for my working with Titus in this way was a combination of my wanting to learn more about dog training and to try some things hands-on, and my being in the habit of doing these kinds of things with horses. Also, the motivation to find some ways to help the dogs in the rescue kennels quit some of the more insufferable behaviors and get them to feel better around people was at play. I really dislike handling dogs who jump on me or other people, expect to drag a person around on the leash, and just go bonkers when humans or other dogs enter the scene. As I worked through some of these things over time with different dogs it became obvious to me that since the point of a rescue is to get dogs adopted, what better way is there to improve dogs' chances of getting happy, forever homes than to get them well behaved? And by "well behaved," I mean not just confined into conditioned responses where their bodies behave and their minds are elsewhere, but rather to have the dogs genuinely feeling relaxed and okay to follow what the human presents. That being with the human is truly a wonderful place to be, and that, in turn, creates the kind of behavior that reflects a truly more blissful mindset as a result of the relationship.

By the time Titus and I went along another dozen steps or so and got to the final door blocking us from the outside run, already he was truly tracking where to walk in relation to me while on the leash. He was off to my left side and slightly behind me, and there was a flow to it and a big ol' loop of slack in the leash. Getting to this point so quickly really surprised me. Although, I anticipated that Titus would relapse into his gregarious mindset and run amuk any second. But, I offered him a feel on the slack leash and gave him the freedom to stay with me or go off the rails rather than try to control him by doing something like choking up tightly on the leash.

Approaching the exit door to the outside run, he was content to walk along right where I wanted him to be. As I stopped at the door, Titus looked up at me and sat calmly. This little guy seemed to get the idea to stay with me way quicker than most dogs, and already seemed happy to follow along with what I was presenting. And, there was an okay-ness and relaxation to it showing that his hyper, pent-up feelings also were defused. It was uncanny and unexpected. (I might even have begun to feel just the tiniest bit of endearment to the little rascal.)

I also thought about how, as I often speak about in regards to horses, if we put in a little time up front to get some things well established that it can thwart years, perhaps a whole lifetime, of fussing about with unwanted behaviors. And Titus began to make it look like that upfront investment wasn't going to require a massive amount of time, either.

I opened the door and he followed after me through it on a slack leash. There existed a "sweet spot" feeling between us, as I would call it with horses who find that nice spot I am offering and are able to be right there with me. Once outside with the door closed behind us, I stopped and asked Titus to sit, and he did. I reached down and petted him once and slid the slip lead off over his head. I got the rope clear of his nose and he checked in with me for a moment before shooting off like bullet from a gun down the run. I thought I'd like to work on that a bit and get him to sit calmly until I said "okay," or some such thing to release him, but all-in-all, not bad for our first five minutes together.

And here is where I might be tempted to say, "Well, the little guy has been pent up in that kennel for hours; I'd be bolting around, too!" But I find that, as with horses, we humans use such an excuse to allow the equines' or canines' minds to blast around. It is one thing to exercise and play. It is something different to be mindless of the human and unhinged. I have seen how horses do not feel good when they are working to get away from a person and are boisterous in that mental place. It brings up anxiety and tension. But a person can make a difference and get horses relaxed and calm by getting them mentally present when turning them loose. The same is true with dogs. It is a maniacal, tense, and sort of icky feeling when a dog is prancing at the end of a leash, pulling to get loose, and the person barely gets the leash unhooked before the dog blasts away.

It is a profoundly better feeling to the person and the dog to have the dog calm and relaxed when taking off the leash rather than having one about to bust to go and get away from the person. In fact, I have begun thinking that turning a dog loose does not have to be an act of letting a dog get away from you, but rather that the turning loose, running, and playing can be a situation where the person is part of the positive experience—that a dog can have running and playing a primary focus but the human is happily kept in mind, even if as a secondary thought, but not something to get away from, bounce off of, or smash over.

I've got more to explain about Titus and this outdoor experience we had the first time we were together. First, though, let me take a break while Titus runs around outside and cover another important idea in the next chapter. We'll meet up again with Titus in bit....

Chapter Two

The Signals We Send

Often I discuss with horse folks how horses always are on—that they always are assessing and re-assessing their relationships to us humans. It is not uncommon to see someone go fetch a horse and pretty much pay zero attention to the animal as they lead the horse from the stall or pasture to be tacked up, or otherwise "do something with" the horse. I have witnessed this with back yard horses and horses at multi-million dollar private facilities.

All over the horse world there are barely leadable horses handled by people who have a death grip on the halter; horses who look like high-headed llamas and are barely controllable. Many other horses are not quite so horrible to lead, yet suffer from lacking a relationship with the human that allows for them to pay attention to the person and to be easily guided on a slack lead rope. People often lack the fundamental understanding of how to change that situation to get a horse who is soft, relaxed, and responsive in general, including when being led.

One component to this dilemma is that people sometimes seem not to realize that the moments spent leading a horse are important. If they did, surely more people would tend to them and make some important changes there. It is as if people can think that the time to concentrate on the relationship with a horse begins when entering the arena or round pen or when putting a foot in the stirrup. That the rest of the time, interactions with the horse are unimportant. But we humans are teaching horses something every moment that we spend with them. Horses do not clock out on learning until they pass through a gate into an arena. They are picking up clues about who we humans are and how to interact with us from how a person catches them, halters them, leads them, grooms them, tacks them up, and so on. And every second contributes to establishing the relationship between the horse and the human—so, when a person does get on a horse, that all-encompassing relationship leading up to the riding will dictate in some way how things will go with the riding.

I find that this also is true with the relationship between dogs and people. Every moment that we spend with dogs, they are assessing and re-assessing their relationships to us humans. If we allow a dog to get all wound up and jump on us when we come in from work and are happy to see them, then why do we think that they ought to understand that this behavior is not okay to do at other times, like when they meet other people for the first time? If we allow a dog to drag us along by the leash constantly, why would we expect him suddenly to listen to what we offer when another dog comes into view? The relationship that gets established in all of the little interactions between a person and a dog is what shows up when it is time to get down to doing all the other things, as well.

In the terminology of horse work as I learned it from Harry, we humans do well to get horses in the habit of letting go of their thoughts. This is a deep topic, one that runs through all of my horse books. But to explain it as simply as possible here, when a horse is unable to let go of a thought to go along with what the human is presenting, "there's trouble in the household," as Harry is prone to say. If a horse will let go of whatever he is thinking and get his mind centered up in the moment with the human, then the horse becomes able to relax and be available to be directed. But when a horse is unable to let go of what he is thinking, that becomes the spot where trouble arises, otherwise he would be happy to follow what the human presents and there would be no trouble. The same can be said of a dog...if a dog would be fine with letting go of a thought to do something undesirable, like jumping on people, barking at the door when people enter, dragging a person on the leash, etc., then those problems would not exist and the dog could be content in the interactions that we present.

This is one of those topics that can be approached from many different angles but let me start with one of the most capable dogmen I know, herding dog trainer and Border Collie breeder, Jack Knox. And let's start with a rather basic thing—as with horses—leading the critter from point A to point B.

Jack teaches herding dog clinics, and the ones that I have attended all have had examples of dog owners getting dragged along on a leash by their dogs. On more than one occasion, I have witnessed Jack break from the stock work to address how a dog is handled on the leash. I am sure that Jack only addresses this because it matters. And I am guessing that while people are there at the clinics to get their dogs going better at herding, it is clear that having a dog leading on a slack leash means that the dog is following what the human is presenting and has let go of the thought to pull away from the person.

I remember distinctly Jack saying to a clinic-goer who had entered the arena with a tight death grip on the leash close to the dog's collar, "There's a reason why they put the handle at the end of the leash."

Jack Knox and me surrounded by his Border Collies at one of Jack's herding dog clinics.

The owner handed the leash to Jack and Jack immediately gave the dog the freedom of some slack in the leash. The dog took off and he hit the end of the leash, and Jack added a well timed bump to it along with a gruff sounding couple of words, “Hey you!” The dog took notice, but then tried again to lead Jack off at a good rate of speed, and the same thing unfolded. In about 25 seconds, that dog had a completely different understanding of the relationship between him and the person on the other end of the leash. Jack then easily led the dog by holding only the handle at the end of the leash, and there was a nice loop of slack between him and the dog. The dog was attentive to Jack, and yet I noticed that the dog had his eyes on the sheep in the arena. The dog was keeping in touch with where Jack was and where he should be in relation to Jack even when his eyes were on the sheep across the way, and the slack never came out of that leash. Jack sorted that deal out with the dog just that fast. I thought about how the owner probably had fought on and on with the dog for months or even years without getting a change in that situation.

The part of this that I think is a really big deal is to point out that the dog in this example also went from rather frenzied to being quite calm and relaxed, walking or standing with Jack. The dog had let go of thinking about being elsewhere so strongly that “there was trouble in the household” and found being primarily attentive to Jack a very good place to be.

When seeing this kind of change, I ask myself what changed? Not the place nor the people or dogs around nor the activities. All of those things remained the very same, just the person on the end of the leash and what he did changed. And that made all the difference in the dog’s mindset and thus his behavior.

So, how does one develop the ability to have that kind of

positive effect on dogs? That's what I am seeking to answer. I long to be able to get the kind of changes in dogs that I do with horses.

At one of Jack's clinics I remember having a conversation with someone who had been attending those clinics for many years. She made a comment after Jack took a few moments to get someone's dog leading better as described above: "Jack takes hold of our dogs, makes some gruff interactions with them, and then they would rather be with him than with us! Look, that dog is happy, lying down right at his feet, and we don't get that."

I got the sense that this person marveled at the fact that owners being nice to their dogs because they want their dogs to love them and do things with them did not produce dogs that worked stock well, behaved well, or even led well. And that being a bit sharp with a dog in a well timed way, surprisingly to some, had the desired effect of producing a dog who wants to be with you, relaxes, and comes easily along with a person.

And this is the very thing that I see at times with volunteers and rescue dogs. Volunteers want the dogs to love them, and they feel sorry for the dogs' past situations with humans, and they tend to express their deep affection towards these dogs by being very "nice" to them. It is obvious that in both cases, with Jack and his clinic-goers and the rescue volunteers, the people genuinely do love those dogs. Who would give so much time and resources if it were not a labor of love? But the thing is, what we humans often think of as being nice to a dog at times is setting them up to not understand how they can be relaxed and calm, and willingly follow a human. And the magic of this, as is the case with horses, is in the timing of what we do as much as in our actions themselves.

Being nice to a dog isn't really being nice to a dog when we either "excite their minds," as Jack sometimes says, or we allow them to get mentally down a wrong trail, whether that be acting wildly, fearfully, or in whatever way ignoring us when we are interacting with them. As with horses, it seems clear to me that dogs are learning from us all the time whether we humans realize it or not. Maybe in our own excitement to see our dog after a day at work, we come home and we get the dog all jazzed up right when we walk in the door. A time or two of that and the next thing we know, when we walk in the door the dog is spinning circles, jumping on us, barking, and maybe that's too much now and the person has to defend himself from the over-exuberance. But, it was the person who trained that dog to behave that way, unintentionally, because at first it seemed that the dog was so very happy to see the person and the person was happy to greet the dog.

I think it is true that the dog can be just as happy to see a person walking in the door from work without jumping on the person or spinning circles. I would go so far as to say that being amped up—even "happily" amped up—is stressful to a dog. "Good" stress or "bad" stress, they both seem to have an ill effect on the creatures and certainly are not relaxed and tranquil states of mind and body. If we discourage over-the-top behavior consistently from the outset with our dogs, and stay consistent with that theme going forward, then we can support a good mindset and behavior in them. And, this can cause our leadership in the relationship to have a positive effect on them.

So what does it look like to set this up? This is where my own study takes me. I am fascinated with how to get dogs—a variety of dogs with a range of personalities, ages, and experiences—to have better relationships with humans and thus better behavior.

First, to my understanding with horses, it is getting a change of thought that leads to a change of feeling that leads to a change of behavior. This means that first, if this also holds true for canines, we must get a change of mind in the dog.

The previous chapter on Titus the terrier is a great example of this. When I approached Titus's kennel the first time, he was jumping, barking, and generally spazzing out. In his previous experiences with people, having his mind all excited, his feelings amped up, and his behavior gregarious got him out of the kennel. And he was running the show from that point on with people. But by not opening the door during his frenzied state, Titus reassessed his situation, and that is done by thinking. As he thought his way through this new situation, he calmed down and he didn't feel so wound up. And that in turn was visible in his behavior that shifted from maniacal to standing and then sitting with some calmness. Then he was able to get released from the kennel—a great reward for the little fella. Consistency with such a deal over time ought to produce a dog who thinks about interactions with humans rather than one who just reacts and throws out a range of behaviors reflexively. One would hope that with consistency over time, the Tituses of the world would find calmness at the kennel door and a calm and less stressful way of life.

And here I come up against a spot between humans and equines and canines that I have contemplated for a long time—that our interactions with horses and dogs can bring about conditioned responses or true willingness in those relationships. This study certainly complicates things further and needs its own chapter....

Chapter Three

Conditioned Response vs. Willing Partnership

Discerning between a conditioned response and a willingness in horses is critically important to getting the best possible relationship. I constantly work to help horse people recognize the difference and to understand how to build willingness into their equine relationships. It followed naturally as I worked with my Belgian Malinois/German Shepherd cross Ellie Mae and other dogs over the years that I looked to see if the same or similar principles hold true. They do.

One horse example to demonstrate this is the use of a rein. If a rider sits atop a horse and wants the horse to take a step with the front right foot to the right, use of the rein is generally how that gets accomplished. It may seem incredibly basic—engage the right rein and the horse steps his right front foot to the right. But why does this work and how does this very straightforward arrangement get sidetracked from a real, conscious communication to an auto-pilot conditioned response?

So often I see this kind of rein/step working as a conditioned response. The rider engages the right rein and the horse steps the front end to the right. The rider releases the right rein and voila, there you have it. But, I see this happening with the horse's head high, the back tight, the horse even may be looking hard back to the left in the opposite direction the rider is asking him to step as he steps to the right to the command of the rein. The horse moves with a body as rigid as a board when stepping. This is not how a happy, willing horse moves.

A willing horse, when the right rein is engaged, steps to the right. But the willing horse's head stays plumb on the end of the neck as the horse turns to look to the right, his mind clearly engaging with the right rein as he thinks and then steps to the right. The head remains low, the neck and back soft, and a bend is present along the neck. The horse is willing to think with the rein and then has a willingness to take the lateral front step to the right. He is balanced to get the job done efficiently, softly, and without resistance.

By contrast, if there is a conditioned response underlying the right front step, the application in horses is what I term "mechanical." A person uses the right rein to produce a discomfort to the horse and "make" the right step happen. This is not the same thing as offering a feel on the right rein for the horse to follow. One approach uses the rein as a communication device, the other as more of a mechanical device.

With the latter, the horse knows it is best to just step to the right or suffer the consequences of discomfort, so he does, even reluctantly and/or mindlessly. I have discovered that there are similar scenarios that play out with dogs.

My friend Jack Knox fascinates me with his approach to training dogs. Training herding dogs, Border Collies in particular, is his main work. He has dominated many trials (herding dog competitions) over the years and stays busy teaching herding dog clinics all over the United States. I immediately was captivated by Jack's approach when witnessing him work Border Collies on sheep at his clinics. And from what I gathered talking to Jack and others at those clinics, it seems that Jack has a reputation in the herding dog world as being a bit of a maverick with his approach to training.

Jack originally hails from Scotland and has lived in the United States now for many decades. In hearing about the differences to his approach to training I am thinking that it may be a combination of his own discoveries of what works commingled with a way of working dogs that he brought with him from Scotland where he began his understanding of herding dog work by herding sheep with old timers. Trial by fire rather than trial by "trials," one might say. The act of training solely for a sport, as is so prevalent today, is different from training/working an animal on a job.

Take cutting horses. Can you go work cows on a ranch with a horse who only has been exposed to cutting in a cutting horse competition training barn? Well, that depends. If that horse never has worked on a ranch before, it might be a total wreck. The experience of being out and around a ranch engaged in ranch work is a world away from being kept in stalls, put on automatic walkers, and put onto cows in a pen for a few minutes of training a day with a guy spurring the horse this way and that way. If the horse works mainly off of very conditioned responses, then the bigger dynamic of activity on the ranch may put him at a loss. But then again, it may be possible to train a horse to be with you in such an environment as a cutting training barn so that he is able to be mentally present with the rider and be able to take to some ranch work right away. I would venture to guess that the conditioned response horse is more prone to come uncorked when put into a position where the conditions are different from what he is used to—thrown into the deep end of the pool regarding the horse's experience, training, and emotional situation.

I attended a herding dog trial here in Virginia where an interesting thing happened that illustrates what I am trying to say. The competition was comprised entirely of dogs who were trained solely for competition—they were owned by people who, if they had flocks of sheep at home at all, did so just to work the dogs in preparation for trialing—except for one man and his Border Collie. These two were a working pair whose job day-in and day-out was working cattle in a feed lot. In fact, I overheard that they never had worked sheep before. The fella just wanted to give a trial a try for fun, so they entered the competition. These two outscored the others. But even if they had not impressed the judges, my novice eyes were able to see clearly an easy, natural flow to their work moving the sheep around that was not present in any of the others.

The reason for the difference had to be their real working relationship. They were on the job together; it was a way of life for them rather than (how can one say it?) a more artificial application of herding. And I bet they could have herding anything—sheep, cows, runner ducks, goats, gazelles, a kindergarten class at recess—effectively because of that togetherness and second nature ability to know where to be to get the job done together. I love thinking about that, and that is what I want in a relationship with a dog. And I wonder just how good such a connection between a human and a dog can get?

Back to Jack and the Border Collie trial world. Jack is prone to boil down his approach to working dogs to a single statement: "Don't try to make the right; correct the wrong." If you are familiar with Scottish accents, I hear Jack's clearly when I write those words. I've likewise heard him give the advice: "Give your dog the freedom to be wrong (but, of course, correct the wrong)."

So, what does this mean? Or, what does this look like in herding? And how does this agree or disagree with my horsemanship and what I've learned from Harry and horses?

Back to the trialing discussion. I hear from some of Jack's students about the current state of herding dog trials that it seems today most judges and winning trainers are producing and rewarding "push button" dogs. This refers to dogs who are extremely controllable. These dogs are micromanaged to the point that they have been trained to follow every command the person gives, even to the point of overriding their own innate herding dog instincts when working stock. One may see, for example, a dog looking at the handler rather than keeping his eyes on the sheep showing the extent to which the dog has been trained to depend on the human's guidance rather than using his own instincts to herd. Jack seems to have an aversion to this kind of training that no doubt flows from his understanding of, and deep respect for, the well bred Border Collie's natural ability to herd.

Border Collies want to herd stock and they carry in the fiber of their beings the primal desire to do so. The greatest reward for well bred Border Collies truly seems to be for the human to get out of the way and let them herd. Still, Jack is shaping how the dogs work the stock. The dog may not possess the big picture of the purpose of a herding operation to know where there sheep need to go or what exactly needs to happen with

Jack Knox works a Border Collie with sheep in the round pen during a clinic in Virginia.

them along the way. A mob of sheep may need to be stopped and held in place or some sheep may need to be "shed" (removed from the group), etc. Also it can be that a dog gets carried away and wants to "grip" (bite) the sheep or crowd them too much, or otherwise run amuck. In Jack's hands, the dogs are given the chance to see if initially they can work the sheep in a desirable way and when they get to heading out of bounds, only then does he intervene to correct them.

To my way of thinking, for a correction to work, the dog must be available to hear the person to thereby adjust the "wrong" actions. If the dog isn't hearing the person, then there can be no communication between the dog and the person. So, the correction must be well timed and its intensity must be dialed in with the correct amount of oomph to be most effective. If a person is late making a correction, then the dog already has gone on to something else and will not understand what the correction relates to. If a correction is too soft, then the dog will not really "give" to the handler, and I think of this as a mental giving, as the mental aspect controls the behavior. If the correction is too strong then the person may overwhelm the dog and cause some issues like getting the dog's attention too far away from the stock and the job at hand and putting worry into the dog that need not be there.

This certainly has parallels to my horsemanship, and I recognized this right away when I watched my first Jack Knox clinic. This seems to overlap with the idea of having a horse's mind centered and available so that a request can be heard. Again, it points to the difference between willing and mechanical as discussed in an earlier chapter.

In my attempts to understand Jack's training and to reconcile it with my unavoidable comparisons to horsemanship, I asked Jack, "How to you handle training a puppy?" I wondered what he did from the very beginning to get his dogs willingly with him.

And when I say "willingly with him," I should share my experience of walking with Jack and a dozen of his Border Collies at once. The scene felt like I was walking along in a cloud of Border Collies as we strolled in an alfalfa field. The black and white creatures surged and flowed like a flock of birds all around us as they tended to their dog business. Every so often one would head out in one direction or another quite far afield and Jack simply calling the dog's name was all that was required to get him or her back into the pack.

Occasionally, a couple dogs would play a little rough, usually a younger dog pushing the envelope with an older dog from what I could tell, and Jack needed only to make a slight noise and the two would quit and go happily about other dog dealings. Jack was the center of awareness, the nucleus of this cell, quite literally the leader of the pack. Seeing these dogs all yielding and remaining attentive to Jack captivated me, and being right there among them allowed me to feel the interactions first hand. There was no fear in the dogs towards Jack, no overbearing control in the handling—it played out exactly as Jack offers as advice to others: "Don't try to make the right; correct the wrong." These dogs had freedom, freedom to do whatever they chose to do, and I felt that individual independence and "happiness." And yet, they were completely willing to yield to Jack's offer of a correction without any discernable stress or animosity. Jack answered my question about how he dealt with puppies with his typical succinctness: "All I need from a pup is for him to know his name and know how to take a correction."

Of course, I tried to pry more from Jack about this. But, it really did start to make sense after spending a little time watching him work dogs of all ages, that that statement does sum it up. If a dog recognizes when you are speaking to him and he knows how to take a correction, then there is pretty much nothing you can't accomplish with a puppy or a dog. The dog can go about life following his own interests and the person will shape his behavior by allowing the rights and correcting the wrongs. If handled well, the corrections need not be worrisome to a dog, but quite the contrary, it seems that they even can provide some boundaries and understanding that help allow a dog to feel supported and know where he stands in the relationship to the person and the world at large.

In Harry's nomenclature with horses, I think similarly of this as getting a change of thought. With horses, what gets people in trouble is when a horse has a thought and we present something else and the horse can not let go of his thought to go along with ours. If a horse was willing to go let go of thinking about his buddies at the barn, for example, then a person would be able to ride that horse away from the barn with the horse being relaxed and directable. If he can not, then tension rises and things like crookedness, prancing, and even more dramatic behaviors like bucking can occur. It seems to me that this applies to dogs, as well. Take herding dogs. If a Border Collie is unable to let go of the thought of gripping a sheep then he is not available to be fully guided by the handler. In my mind, Jack's reference to "correct the wrong" has at its core getting the dog to let go of a thought to be available to shift gears and be more with the person on the task at hand.

I am trying to sort out if there are some differences to horses here. I wonder, for instance, is the dog keeping track of the handler relatable to the horse keeping track of what the rider (or a person doing ground work) is offering. Or, with a horse, is a person directing more of the time than Jack would expect one to do with a Border Collie on sheep?

With herding dogs, Jack might get a dog to "give" (let go of that unhelpful thought) to then turn the dog loose to his own thoughts again to work the sheep, but he would not want the dog to loose track of him completely. There is a balance between the dog the sheep and the handler that is at play even when the dog has the freedom to have his sheep.

I suppose there is a correlation here to, say, a cutting

horse. If the horse "has cow," as they say, then a person might just be up there in the saddle letting the horse do his thing and only offer some guidance if the horse gets off balance on the job.

Here is where a person (like me) starts to come up against a bit of a tough deal. I think of often quoted and respected horsemen like Ray Hunt. People always are quoting Ray, and in my equestrian journalist role of interviewing scores of horse people over the years I have come to notice that many of them start right from the beginning of an interview talking about their time with Ray. And Ray was quite influential and said some things that are very quotable, so that's really not a surprise. One of those sayings attributed to Ray goes something like, "They know when you know, and they know when you don't know." The tough part of this is that who really can know what Ray meant? I find that Ray often left people to figure things out for themselves rather than to elaborate. And I can say from experience that trying to find the right words to describe a horsemanship concept is very difficult, and words strung together have a different effectiveness from person to person.

But, that doesn't mean that the exercise of considering what a capable hand meant by what was said isn't helpful. A person probably can be off the mark of what someone like Ray meant when he said what he said but still glean some benefit from thinking about it. I won't pretend to know what Ray meant exactly by the remark above. But I do know that it comes to my mind when I am working with horses. In my experience, "They know when you know, and they know when you don't know," often means that horses know when a person is seeing that they are taking their thoughts elsewhere, or not.

When I work with a horse I am meeting for the first time, sometimes the changes can be quite dramatic to the positive. This often is due to the fact that the horse never has had anyone recognize that he is away mentally when a person goes to interact with him. Get a horse's brain lined up there with you and it is amazing some of the challenging behaviors that simply disappear. Sometimes, the awareness of a person realizing where a horse's focus is and isn't can be rather disturbing to a horse. At other times, it seems a horse says, "Thank you! I have been waiting for someone to recognize my challenges and help." But whatever the result, that quote has been helpful to me because it explains to my way of thinking that a horse can recognize a person's abilities and that in turn can influence how the horse thinks, and thus behaves. And if a person doesn't "know," then the relationship with the horse will be more difficult because the person is missing something critical to establishing a deeper relationship.

I think that this similarly applies to what Jack offers his clinic goers. "Don't try to make the right; correct the wrong" is a pretty simple statement. As with Ray's quote, I may never really know what Jack means through-and-through, but it is helpful to try. And there may be many layers to discover as to how it can be applied. On the surface, there may be a more mechanical application of it—"No dog; don't do that." But there also may be deeper truths that it points to. I think that it is possible to get a dog to change his behavior on the surface without really getting a deeper mental change. What is meant by correction? Is it just getting a behavior to stop? Is it getting the behavior to switch from one thing to another? Does it mean to get a mental yielding in which the unwanted behavior evaporates as a by-product of a true mental yielding to a person?

I contemplate (and perhaps complicate) these things, and I may offer less certainty to you as to their answers than I would like even as I share the direction that I find myself going with them. But, ultimately the proof is with the dogs and horses themselves. They let us humans know when something works or not. If we train ourselves to (as Harry says) recognize the "motions that go with good emotions and the motions that go with sorry emotions," then we can become better readers of what a dog's behavior is telling us. What does a worried dog look like? What does a dog look like who is willing or unwilling to follow what we offer for direction? Do we see improvements when we try this or that?

The best horse and dog trainers most certainly are those who have excellent observation skills. If nothing else, I can say with certainty that my advancement in horsemanship is directly related to seeing in better ways what is going on with the horses right in front of me. Noticing things that were there all along but that I just couldn't see, and now that I see them I couldn't unsee them if I wanted to, they seem so obvious. I am finding that the same is true with working dogs. And that reminds me of a particularly amazing and quick change in the worst case of a fearful dog that I ever have seen. But that's a whole other chapter....

Chapter Four
Kona and Marcy

Dogs sometimes arrive worried and skittish to rescue kennels since the backgrounds of rescue dogs all-too-often are lamentably peppered with sad stories. Neglect, abusive humans, and who knows what all give some of these mutts good reasons to be dubious of people. One of the big jobs of rescue animal volunteers is to help acclimate these frightened critters to kind and loving people, and to alleviate their stress and worry when possible. As with horses, dogs are experiential learners. You can not lecture a dog or provide one a text book to read and expect learning to occur. The person must be in the moment as issues come up with the dog and then re-direct the outcome for the benefit of the dog to prove to the canine that the world can be this other, more positive way.

One of the worst cases I've witnessed so far also proved to be one of the quickest turn-arounds of any troubled dog I have seen. Kona was a medium sized mixed breed female. When she came into the kennel, I heard from Carol a lot of the buzz about how badly worried this dog was—an extreme case who cowered in the corner of her kennel. It was all that the volunteers could do to drag her outside to do her business, and there seemed to be no progress with her after some days. When I heard that the dog had been taken into rescue from her previous situation and was with a person trying to help her for a couple of months before arriving to the kennel I thought, "Well, this must be a pretty damaged dog—if a change can occur in her, how would a person get that accomplished? And how much time it might take?"

It wasn't long before I was helping Carol do the mid-day shift at this kennel. The kennel structure was a prefabricated building and technically, it had six kennels. Realistically, they were so small that every two kennels were opened up together to make a total of three kennels. The inside kennels sported dog doors that the dogs can open themselves to access "outside" pens included in the prefabricated building that are under roof and have chain link fencing. These outer pens have doors that people can open to allow the dogs access to a large fenced-in outside play area.

Helping Carol at the kennel that day, I saw this petrified, new dog for myself. Carol entered Kona's kennel slowly. The dog was balled up on her bed, looking away. Carol moved very cautiously and sat down on the bed beside her. Kona never looked in her direction. The dog's deeply furrowed brow and diverted distant eyes clearly revealed profound worry. This dog was consumed with concern and just lay there quaking awaiting a horror show of some kind to descend upon her.

After a few minutes of petting Kona softly, with no visible change in the dog's expression, Carol invited me into the kennel with them to see how it would go.

With horses, I find that tiptoeing around them seems to

send a message from the human that indeed, there is something to worry about. This often prolongs and even amplifies the worried behavior. So, often I just approach horses matter-of-factly to prove to them that nothing bad is about to befall them. And, quite the contrary, that I can approach them even with my hands waving above my head, flipping the lead rope around, and that such haphazard displays are no big deal. Soon, most horses get to where they understand that they may relax around me—or any person—and that such movements are not a threat.

I had a suspicion the same might be true for dogs. But Kona was incredibly worried and I was not about to experiment with that at this point with her, so I entered the kennel as softly as I could manage.

Carol still sat on the squatty dog bed with Kona, gently petting her and said that I should try to pet her. When I very slowly, and with the kindest feel I could manage, reached out to touch the dog, she jumped from the bed and crammed herself into one corner of the tiny kennel and peed as she went. This was an extreme worry case. The other thought I had initially was that I was glad that she was all flight and no fight and showed no threatening behavior. Kona just wanted to disappear into the floor and mentally withdrew herself as far away as she could manage.

I asked Carol what she knew about the this dog? That was when I heard the somewhat shocking news that the dog had been in the care of someone trying to help her for a couple of months. There was no doubt that this person had been kind to Kona, so how could she be so over-the-top worried still after two months? I wondered why none of the kindness afforded a dog this submissive and worried had brought about some better results than what I was witnessing in that kennel. Then Carol mentioned that the person who had her recently reportedly had pretty much just given the dog lots of treats to try to get her to come around to having a better experience with people. I wondered if perhaps feeding the treats when the dog cowered and felt horrible served only to reward the worry for ill feelings with food, building the problem in firmer? It was hard to say for sure, but I could see that the dog in front of me was extremely apprehensive, concerned, anxious, and troubled all rolled into a pitiful pile of dog curled up in a corner of the kennel.

I asked Carol if she objected to me getting a slip lead and taking the dog outside. Carol, not having much luck at getting her to feel any better at this point, and knowing that Kona had to go outside, said okay, and she went to tend to other dogs.

I stepped out of the kennel, grabbed Kona's slip lead that was draped over a hook on the wall, and then stepped back in. Kona evaded me by scurrying as hard as she could and pressing herself to the back corner of the kennel in what only can be described as complete terror. I had to question what had befallen this sweet little dog to get this kind of ill feeling established about humans.

I got to thinking about Kona's recent experiences. Clearly all of the nice, cautious, loving, tiptoeing handling Kona had received had made little difference if she still behaved like this after many weeks of that kind of treatment. Something else had to be tried if a change was to be made in Kona, so I figured that I would approach her more matter-of-factly like I would a horse. I went right over to her in my normal, easy going way. She already was cowering, so it wasn't like acting normal around her was going to make things any worse. I placed the slip lead over her head.

Luckily this dog, as mentioned before, did not have an aggressive streak in her. Another dog might have gone into fight mode when cornered and come after me when I went to place the slip lead over her head, but none of that was in Kona. Next, to get her up and out of the kennel I quite literally had to drag her into the aisle way and out the human's door to the spacious play yard adjacent to the kennels.

Once outside, and at Kona's first opportunity, she ran away from me and hit the end of the leash in one direction. I just kept walking along as if I did not notice this, providing the feel of a place for her to be walking with me. In other words, I went along leading as I would with any dog, and if she found the spot to be walking along beside me, there would be the reward of a sweet spot between us where things would flow and she could just easily come along on a slack leash. Then, realizing that I was not stopping when she crumpled to the ground, she sprang up and flew past me in another direction attempting to flee and hit the end of the leash over there. This continued around the play yard. Finally, I stopped and thought about the situation, looking at pitiful Kona and longing to find a way to help her.

With horses, a helpful approach when working to get one to lead who is worried about the human that I picked up from Harry is to in some way get the horse mentally centered up with me, give a quick pet on the face to see if the horse can stay with me, and then walk off and see if the horse can connect and follow along with me. The quick pet on the face provides two purposes. The main one is to test to see if the horse really is with me mentally. If I am able to reach out and stroke a horse down the nose and the horse doesn't duck away or look elsewhere, then the eyes stay on me and the horse truly is focused on me. It only takes one stroke to achieve this. Two or more may work against me and bring about the need for the horse to look or get away from my approaching hand. Second, there can develop a good feeling between us such that the horse may come to appreciate the pet on the face and that helps to get them to hunt up that nice spot between us. This interaction has become second nature to me so I naturally want to do a similar thing with dogs, although I pet the dog's head and not down the canine's nose.

This troubled dog was not helped by my leading, stopping, petting her, and walking off again. Off I would go, connected to her by a leash. She would be lying on the ground. The slack would come out of the leash and I kept walking until she felt the pull of the leash and was convinced to get up and reluctantly follow, not coming into a harmonic position with me in the least. If she walked along at all, I'd stop and pet her on the head even though she recoiled from my reaching. Then, as with a horse, I walked off again and repeated the scenario. In the past, I had enjoyed quite a bit of luck doing this with a variety of different dogs while volunteering with Carol the rescue kennels, but this troubled critter was way too worried about the human for this to come through. She stayed out at the far end of the leash and cowered something fierce.

Then I got an idea.

Again, experience with horses helped to formulate this idea in my mind. A new dog had just arrived at the kennel. This was a magnificent female dog named Marcy, a Burna-Doodle—that is, a mix of Bernese Mountain Dog and Poodle. Marcy stood waist high to me with thick, curly black, white, and reddish hair and solid bone, quite the contrast to pale white Kona who was smaller and fine boned. Also dissimilarly, Marcy was a very happy sort of dog who had mastered several basic commands and was well leash trained. Not a typical rescue dog, Marcy had been "owner surrendered" due to circumstances with her owner and not otherwise related to any problems with her. Marcy showed a twinkle in her eyes (when you could see them through the hair), and she was only a year old.

With horses, if I work with a "sticky" one who is difficult

Working one horse from another (here my mare Mirage is my saddle horse and we are ponying my two-year-old Newly) got me thinking that I might be able to use one dog to help another.

to get thinking and moving forward and there is a capable saddle horse available, sometimes ponying the sticky one from the other is very helpful. The saddle horse can help build confidence in the other one as well as provide an opportunity for the horse to get used to a human directing things from above where we sit when riding. Thinking about that, I got the notion to get the big, playful, good natured, leadable Berna-Doodle out of her kennel to help the timid and terrified mutt with her confidence and freeing her mind up to walk with me on leash.

I set things up so that Marcy was to my far left on a leash and Kona was between Marcy and me, also on a leash. I held both leashes in my left hand. As I took off walking at a good clip, the fuzzy Berna-Doodle tracked right along with me, ready to go. The worried Kona, sandwiched between us, almost immediately fell in with our forward energy and for the first time she came along willingly. It was amazing to see and feel the immediate change in Kona.

Repeating this several times, Kona was thinking and going right along with Marcy and me, then she'd stop with us and I would pet Kona on the head, and off we'd go again, in unison. Kona's head came up as she took in the world, her eyes brightened, and for the first time I saw the curious dog inside Kona come out of that shell of fear she had carried around constantly. Kona's entire posture and disposition changed and she became engaged with us.

We three stopped, started, trotted all over that play yard, and stopped again. I was petting Kona at the stops and she would look right at me now, another first for her. That terrified dog made the biggest change I had ever seen in a dog, and shifted for the better in by far the shortest time of any dog I had worked with before. It was nothing short of amazing, but it got even better.

Things went so well so rapidly that soon I put big, happy Marcy up in her kennel and kept working with Kona to see how it would go—if the new found freedom, focus, and good feel between us would remain if it went back to just the two of us working together. To my astonishment, Kona continued to follow my lead and came along right with me just as she had when Marcy had been with us. Me being me, I wondered if this change really was some kind of a sudden and real breakthrough, so I decided to go a step further.

I kept Kona following along with me on the leash. When I would stop, she would stop, I would pet her on the head, she took it fine, and then I would walk off again with her right there in the sweet spot on a slack leash following fine. While doing this, we got to one corner of the play yard. We turned around and then headed back the other way. About a third of the way across the pen I stopped and Kona did, too. I reached down and petted her on the head and she accepted the gesture with relaxation and a pleasant look. I scratched her gently on the neck and deftly slipped the rope lead over her ears, past her snoot, and off her head completely. The I stood up and walked off just as I had been doing before.

Kona now was free. As I walked off with Kona at liberty to go wherever she wanted to, Kona willingly came along and walked right in step with me tracking just where I wanted her off to the left side and a little behind me.

I was thrilled!

I stopped and she stopped. I petted her once and then I walked off again. She looked happy and came right along with me, no leash. We walked all over that yard together with her lose and she was right with me...it was magical. I stopped the work on that amazing note and returned her to her kennel.

Not every worried dog has so quick a turn-around to get feeling better about humans and be able to function as a more relaxed and happy animal. But Kona proved to me that day that it is possible, at least sometimes, to get a remarkable change for the better in a troubled dog quickly. She remains one of the ultimate experiences for me, going from the most fearful, cowering, peeing herself dog to a blooming, happy dog moving gracefully and at ease with me, and in far less than an hour, It proved that, at least in a case like Kona's, that my thinking and some of the feeling and timing from my horse work can translate in some helpful ways of working with dogs. And the real hero in this deal was Marcy.

Experimenting to see if using Marcy's okayness with humans could help gain Kona's confidence was such a successful ice-breaker in this instance, it was a lesson of its own. The idea of having a capable dog to help work with other dogs had not occurred to me before, and now the idea very much intrigues me. From that point on, I have had in mind to look more into using one dog to help work with others, and maybe getting my next dog to be savvy to that kind of work. Having witnessed this amazing turn-around, I can say with confidence that the change would not have happened so rapidly without a dog like Marcy to assist in the work. And helping a severely troubled abandoned rescue dog is, well...deeply satisfying.

So, what happened next? Marcy, not surprisingly, already had been adopted by the time she came to the rescue kennels. She was being held for a few days as her new owner got ready to bring her home. Kona, I was told, made a profound and lasting change that day. After that one session, volunteers reported that she remained out of her shell and made great progress quickly becoming what they said was a "normal" dog. And before long, Kona was adopted to a forever home and it seems all went well.

I saw Kona one other time at the kennel before she was adopted and she was playing happily with another dog and a volunteer, loose in the play yard. It was a delightful sight!

Chapter Five
Why Being Nice Alone Doesn't Always Work

Of the several lessons I recorded in my mind from working with Kona that day, one really remains a regular reflection as I ruminate on how to better train dogs. That is how all of the being nice to Kona and giving her treats for many weeks that reportedly occurred ahead of our first experience together did not make a change for the better with her. What really helped was working with her directly and bringing up her worrisome situations to then cause a change in her thinking to get her past her problems. And the big ice breaker proved to be getting Marcy to help free up her mind to the possibility that going along with a human can work out okay.

Being nice and hoping a dog will like us obviously is not

enough in some instances to bring about positive and lasting changes. Why is this? Why wouldn't a nice person and lots of treats help a terribly worried dog like Kona break through to a better mindset?

As mentioned in the previous chapter, I have a hunch that treats and loving gestures can be mis-timed. That can reinforce the opposite of what we would like to accomplish. For instance, let's say a dog is worried about stepping onto a tile floor. The owner sees this concern as the dog stands on a carpeted floor looking sort of sideways at the tile floor. The owner tries to defuse the dog's worry by comforting and hugging him, telling him he's fine, loving on him, and giving him treats just as the dog is feeling worried about considering stepping onto the tile floor. The dog may connect feeling worried about the tile floor and not stepping onto it with some pretty awesome praise, love, and food. That timing may build the worry about the tile floor into a lasting and very large issue. Whereas, if the person sees the concern in the dog for the tile floor and then helps support the dog to step onto it and then pets the dog for making the breakthrough and overcoming the fear, then a loving gesture should reinforce in the dog to not be worried about the tile floor.

Dogs are experiential learners, and this is a fact that I state frequently about horses. Both live in the moment and do not have the ability to take in a verbal lesson or read a book or see a video and learn something from it. Rather, we must set up experiences that bring up the issues needing to be worked on and then work on them in real-time, and hope that things go well and progress to positive results.

This also means that we bring up the very behaviors we want to help overcome. One big point that I have learned when working with horses is to not get emotional. Very often, people take what horses and dogs do personally when it is not personal with the animal. The animal is trying to be safe in the best way he or she can manage and is in the moment. People are capable of holding a grudge and wanting to exact revenge. But a horse or a dog never gets up one morning, kicks or bites a persons, and says, "Hey buddy, that's for feeding me late that time last week." And if a person gets angry, fearful, or is in some way quite emotional when working on getting a positive change in behavior, the animal does not comprehend this emotional state but feels the amplification of the interaction and it can increase confusion and worry. It may make a person seem all the more suspicious, thus putting another road block in the way of getting a positive change.

As I work to comprehend what I can about pack mentality with dogs, there is an interesting point I have heard that also may come into play here. Dogs, it seems, will ostracize and sometimes even attack or kill members of their own pack if an individual's behavior becomes unstable. This also can happen with injured or older dogs. The general belief is that this likely is a natural mechanism for keeping the pack safe. An unstable or less capable individual can endanger the whole pack. It stands to reason that behavior from us that seems erratic, including emotionally driven responses with dogs, may qualify for getting us removed from the pack.

Following this line of thinking, I try to be both very consistent and judicious with my requests and responses with dogs, and be unemotional about it. We humans with our big brains can do much to set up our dogs to win and support them when they do come through to a better place.

Back to the question again—so why didn't all of the niceness help Kona before the work with Marcy and me? Looking again at how dogs interact with one another; have you ever seen a dog get another dog to do something and then go find a food treat and give it to him or her? No. It doesn't happen. Harry mentions this about horses, and I see the same point is valid with dogs.

Horses and dogs do not live in positive reinforcement based societies. Rather, they interact with one another through a feel. When things are in balance with other members of their own species and the world around them, that is the reward they seek—that sweet spot. And when things go sideways, they posture with one another. If that posturing doesn't work, things get physical. Dogs will growl, bite, and fight until one either backs down and there is a willingness to give to the other or there are some terrible injuries or death that settle the issue. So using treats to bribe a dog to do something is a foreign concept to them. When humans do it, there can be results for desired behaviors, but often these are produced through conditioned responses rather than a willing relationship with the person. Any way you slice it, by using praise and treats we are not establishing the kind of relationships that dogs forge with one another. And thinking about it, I find that this is part of the answer to my question about Kona.

Kona, it seems to me, only made a breakthrough and felt better once she comprehended the communication that she had a safe place in a pack. That she was safe to come along and do things with others, and that dogs and people could be part of her pack and that could work out well for her. But getting that change required taking her to a very uncomfortable place, at first. Staying mentally withdrawn in her "comfortable" spot, even with humans being nice and petting her and showering her with treats, would have meant that she never left the cowering corners of her kennel or had much real interaction with people. She had to be forced to leave her comfort zone to find that life could be different from the fearful existence she had embodied.

Reflecting on this amazing change in Kona keeps me tuned into the fact that major change is possible in some troubled dogs when we actively work to help them find new understanding through sometimes simple tasks with good feel and timing.

Meet Stash—she's a Dutch Shepherd owned by my son, Cody Moates, who is a dog trainer in Charlotte, North Carolina. I love this puppy picture, and yes, she did grow into those ears!

Chapter Six
Titus Two

When we last saw Titus back in Chapter One, I had turned him loose in the outside run and off he went to the races!

As mentioned earlier, I enjoy a dog who is capable of relaxing when I go to open a kennel door and who is okay with me entering and getting the slip-lead on his or her head. I also appreciate one who yields to me as I walk first through doors. Add to that list, a loose dog who does not come running up and jump on me. And, back when I was working with rescue dogs at the kennel where I met Titus, there was another behavior that I worked to change when volunteering with those rescue dogs—not allowing the dogs to jump up onto a bench that was located in the outside run.

Anyone familiar with my Facebook page probably is saying, "But Tom, there are photos of Ellie Mae sitting beside you on benches, gliders, chairs, and even a porch swing!"

That is true. But those were instances where I invited her up with me for the photos. She did not lose track of me and just jump up there on her own. The rescue dogs at the kennel tended just to barge right up on the bench out of habit as a by product of running a bit wild and without consideration for the humans occupying the bench—humans who mostly praised and loved them for acting that way and being on the bench with them. I get that people tend to associate this kind of behavior with a dog who loves them and wants strongly to be with them. But the way it often gets handled bothers me because the dog does not check in with the person before hopping up there. The dog may leap onto the bench even before the human has a chance to sit down and get comfortable.

Again, when looking at the adoptability of a rescue dog, it seems that it might be best to err on the side of caution and not train or allow a dog to get onto furniture since a potential adopter may not want a dog who is in the habit of hopping on benches, couches, beds, and chairs. Blocking a dog from hurling himself up onto the bench (and sometimes plowing into the person) without an invite is one of those spots that I am ready to make a correction and get a change of thought.

Now that we were outside in the fenced in area and Titus was free from the confines of the leash, he was ripping around like a wild thing. He ran to the far end, turned around at the fence, and he came running like a gazelle right at me. I felt him bee-lining me with a speed and intent that clearly made jumping on me a very real probability. With the loping dog few feet away from me, I threw up my hand and said, "Aught!" Titus stopped in his tracks a few inches from me, sat, and looked at me intently.

Part of the beauty of the preemptive maneuver certainly was that it prevented Titus's lift off so that he did not jump on (and bounce off of) me. But in that moment, I felt the terrier's mind shift gears. It seemed perhaps to be along the lines of what

Jack says about training dogs, that if you get a correction working then you just correct the wrongs and leave the rights alone. Titus went to thinking, and thinking about me instead of just spazzing around me and jumping on me thoughtlessly. I had a new status, one of importance, and that kind of relationship began taking shape rather quickly.

Before long, I thought about sitting on the bench. Titus went back to flittering about the run doing his own thing. Sure enough, as I went to sit down, here he came at a gallop towards the bench like a fighter jet looking to land on an aircraft carrier. I sat and had just enough time to put a hand up and say, "Aught!" Titus stopped short of jumping on the bench and his butt hit the ground.

"Go git," I said, shooing him away with my hand, and off he went ripping around again.

Soon he circled back and made a second approach. "Titus to tower, I'm approaching the aircraft carrier for a second try," I could hear in my mind. I blocked him again. This time he stopped, sat, and then scootched along in the sitting position closer to me and got up against my right leg. I petting him once on the head, and said, "Go git." Off he went.

This repeated a few times, and it had a nice feel to it. Titus now was not just blasting around wildly. His mind stayed on me more even as he was running around. Now, he was not dismissive of my presence or of considering what I might direct him to do. Even at a distance and with him running about, we were more together than if I had just let him mush into me on the bench or bounce off of me while I was standing.

I stood up and called him over. Titus came eagerly but thoughtfully to me. He loped over, but slowed to a walk on his own as he got close to me and then sat at my feet. I easily placed the slip lead over his head, petting him once, and then I walked off towards one end of the pen. As I stepped off, I presented a spot for him to follow along with me, off to my right side and slightly behind me. He fell right in with me and we walked easily together. I stopped; he stopped and sat without me saying a word. I petted him once and stepped off again. Titus was right with me. I stopped; he stopped. I petted him once and off we went again, together. The feeling was as if we were nearly one, like I work to get going with the horses I lead, and I remained amazed at how quickly the terrier picked up on all of this. It forever changed my bias towards little terriers from the negative to the positive.

In my experience so far, it is rare for a dog to catch onto getting with me so quickly as Titus did that day. But the experience proved to me that such a change is possible. As importantly, it helped me to develop more a feel for working with a dog in this way—a way similar to how I approach horses in similar circumstance, leading, stopping, petting once or twice, walking off again offering a place for the critter to follow along with me.... What an amazing feeling it is when a dog or horse is willingly following along with what I present. And once that kind of relationship gets working in those seemingly small interactions, it feels like all kinds of possibilities open up because the dog is listening and open to trying different things that the person offers.

It wasn't simply that Titus began to "behave" as I wanted him to that produced my unexpected enjoyment when working with him. It was more than that. Titus really looked to me, willingly wanting to know what I directed. He wanted to know what we were going to do next. The quickness with which he let go of his own plans and picked up what I offered was remarkable. In fact, I rarely had felt this in other dogs aside from my long time companion, Ellie Mae.

Chapter Seven
Gladys

I remain uncertain of what all is involved in the pack dynamic, but I do have an example from personal experience that I think provides a good clue to at least one aspect of it: namely, how a capable leader can change a dog's behavior dramatically for the better.

Harry says horses are born ready to follow a capable leader. The question for people then becomes, what is a capable leader for any given horse? And if there is no capable leader around, then a horse finds no alternative but to run the show. It looks to me like this idea overlaps into the dog world.

Gladys was a dog who came to a rescue via a local county dog pound. She clearly had plenty of Belgian Malinois in her. After living with Ellie Mae for over a decade, it is pretty easy to feel out those Malinois traits, like strong mindedness, strong work ethic, and what I call assuming the role of "upper management." Volunteers were talking about many difficulties dealing with Gladys. She was so over the top with toys that it was dangerous to try to get her to quit playing with them and get them away from her. She developed a reputation for being aggressive towards other dogs and had the crew so concerned that a policy was implemented that Gladys had to be kept away from other dogs and not even allowed to be along a chain link fence next to other dogs.

When I began working with Gladys, aside from the toy craziness, I saw none of this behavior. Perhaps I should back up and say that when I began working with her, I approached her the same as I would any other dog. I would get her to sit or lie down before I opened the kennel door. I would place a slip lead on her. Then, at first, as she attempted to lead me out of the kennel, I slapped my leg, got her attention, and then did the leading. This looked a lot like what I described earlier with Titus, and came through pretty quickly, too.

After that initial experience, Gladys always put in an effort to keep me in mind and follow my lead when we interacted. But what I find profoundly interesting is that when Gladys and I were together, she never had any trouble with the other dogs, either. I found that she was so easy to work with and keep right with me that I deliberately ignored the notes to keep her away from shared fences with the other dogs. It just was not an issue. Even if she was sniffing around the play yard with some dog business and moseyed near to a dog or two behind their chain link fences, she usually never seemed to care one lick about them. Very occasionally, I would notice Gladys heading intently towards a dog behind a chain link kennel door, not really going for it but with some intent. All it took was one slight noise from me as a reminder and she would let that thought go and just trot right on past the other dog/s. She readily stayed mentally with me when loose.

Another interesting thing that Gladys presented was that she often would lie down and go belly up. In fact, she was rather ridiculously habitual with this prostrate position. It kinda drove me nuts, especially as I hate auto-pilot responses in horses and dogs, and clearly, the way she flung herself thoughtlessly onto the ground upside-down all the time at my feet showed this to be one.

This submissive behavior seemed to run counter to the otherwise more dominant behavior she presented. I wondered if it was a conditioned response that she had picked up along the way? I worked hard with her over many sessions to get her to lie down without flopping over. I worked on this by asking her to lie down and then approaching her with my hand to pet her. When she flopped over, I withdrew my hand and stood up. Then I would ask her to lie down again. Over time, she got the idea that she only got petted when she would lie down Sphinx style and not if she went belly-up.

This was a really tough habit to break and took a lot of sessions to get working. Of course, she was being handled by many other people, too. So, I was sure that she was getting rewarded with belly rubs for flopping over upside down, reinforcing the old behavior the rest of the time. But we finally did get there. And it was funny to me to watch her begin to do the auto-pilot upside down fling thing and then—suddenly realizing I was there and was not going to reward her for that—catch herself in time to stop the flop and just lie down upright. That cracked me up! But I loved how it showed her shift from auto-pilot thoughtless behavior to thinking about what she was doing. And I am sure that this training time we spent together added to the kind of willing working relationship we enjoyed.

It occurred to me after Gladys had been in the kennel a long time without being adopted that perhaps getting her to do a trick might help her prospects of adoption. I decided to see if I could teach her to roll over. This took very little time. I had

Mirage follows the feel I present and is with me as I direct her thought from a position back a ways where the rider will sit. Mirage's relaxed and soft posture shows her willingness to follow me without feeling the need to take over in the relationship.

taught Ellie Mae to roll over when she was about eight years old, so I had some previous Malinois experience in this department.

The thing about Gladys that really sticks with me, though, is just how different she acted when she was with me compared to when she with some of the other people who were helping to take care of her. The main person interacting with her at any moment made the difference between her demonstrating severely concerning behavior with other dogs (and sometimes people) and her presenting pretty much no trouble whatever. What a radical difference the person working with the dog made with her.

I am convinced that this bipolar exhibition of behaviors resulted from a couple of things. On the one hand, simply establishing clear boundaries and expectations with her right from the start of our relationship allowed her to feel confident and safe with following me. That versus her being with other humans who, in her mind, likely were not considered capable leaders who could keep her safe. Without a capable leader, Gladys took potential threats quite seriously and she had a natural need to take care of them the best way she knew how. This is speculation, but in my mind, it fits the evidence.

And Gladys is a bit if an extreme case as she would "go at it" with a dog through a chain link fence to the point that she and other dogs would get minor injuries from the scuffles. As I mentioned, I never saw this behavior, not even once, when we were together. She always was aware of my presence and looked to me first and knew that aggressive behavior wasn't going to work out for her, nor was it necessary since she was safe if I was around—that I was looking out for her and the other dogs. I think that this is the pack leader kind of situation that gets discussed in training circles sometimes. It makes sense that it would be. But it holds true even in less extreme cases, as with Titus, whose worst crimes were to bounce around the kennel, bark, and want to drag people on the end of a leash. With some boundaries and not letting the shenanigans work out, Titus became a much more relaxed, attentive, and reasonable dog.

I am convinced that dogs feel better, let down, and really thrive when their people prove themselves to be worthy of their submission. And that dogmanship should be all about establishing that kind of relationship. The absence of a capable leader in the human means that dogs have an instinctual need to take care of themselves at the very least, and probably run the pack (even if it is a pack of two), as well. That leads to many problems that people face with their dogs.

Consider this, if a dog happily follows whatever a person asks, how could there be a problem? The dog barks. The person asks him to stop barking and he stops. No problem. The dog goes to chew on the couch. The person says no don't do that and the dog doesn't, and happily goes and finds a toy instead. No problem. It is when a dog is running along with his own thoughts and will not let them go when the person asks that we have a problem. As Jack Knox says, get the dog knowing his name and a get a correction working and you can get most anything working with a dog.

And if the relationship is one where the dog willingly and happily submits to the person's requests, well, it does not get much better than that. But, if a dog is simply conditioned to do or not so something, that is quite a different thing than really wanting to do it because of their relationship with us, as discussed back in Chapter Three. So, let's look a bit more at training and aspects of getting dogs to be those willing partners that we love to have....

Chapter Eight
School's Out

Years ago, Harry did quite a bit of dog training. Harry also did some rodeo clowning and included dogs and other animals that he trained in his acts. I've heard him tell one dog training story in particular at horsemanship clinics to help illustrate the point of how different breeds produce a variety of mindsets and behaviors—for both horses and dogs.

The story goes, Harry was training a Border Collie of his own and a friend had a Lab mix that he asked Harry to work with. Harry went about training these two dogs together. Getting them to sit on a pedestal was part of the training. As Harry wrapped up the training sessions, both dogs were sitting on the pedestal. Harry would release the dogs to have their own free time by saying, "school's out."

When Harry said "school's out," the Border Collie would be gone in a flash, off the pedestal to do something—she already had plans to tend to several things and was eager to get to them. The Lab, on the other hand, would just remain sitting there on the pedestal looking around. Then he'd look around some more. Then he'd look around some more as he began to form some kind of plan of what he might do. Eventually, he'd get down off the pedestal and look around some more. By this time, the Border Collie had ticked five items off her to-do list and was working on a new list.

This is a brilliant illustration of how breed is a factor in behavior and how it effects personality in dogs. It may be worth mentioning here that when searching for the right dog, breed should be a careful consideration for finding a good fit between specific humans, their living arrangements, and dogs. Maybe that seems like a no-brainer, but having seen some mis-matched dogs and people over the years it seems worth a mention.

So, back to the "school's out" idea. This same basic idea is used in other kinds of training, like for police dogs and service dogs. Some info that I came across discussed that with service dogs it is very important to give the dogs definite down time of their own. A service dog has great responsibilities, and those may even be around the clock in some instances. It was reported that this kind of work can be quite stressful on a dog and so it becomes very important that people make allowances for these dogs to have a certain amount of time each day that is just their own to let down. They fare better when they get clear breaks from being on duty.

Typically, it is requested that people not pet service dogs when they are on the job. Some service dogs even wear signs requesting that people not pet them. Not petting a service dog helps the dog to know that he or she is working and needs to be focused on the job. It is pretty easy to understand, for example, that if the dog is working with a blind person, the owner may not even know that the dog is being distracted by someone petting it. If this occurs near a curb, stairs, traffic, or other dangerous places, the person could end up injured due to the dog's distraction.

I've seen videos of drug dogs working, and when they find what they are looking for, the handler gives the dog his or her special toy as a reward. Then, off the dog goes to spend some time chewing and playing with the toy. This seems to be the same kind of thing—even though it is a reward for the dog alerting to drugs, it defines a clear difference between on the task and off.

With herding dogs, one often hears the command from the handler, "That'll do!" It is used when a dog is asked to leave the stock and return full attention to the human, and maybe come all the way back to the person. After a little time at herding dogs clinics, I began to use "that'll do" with Ellie Mae in our everyday activities. It seemed like the perfect verbal command for the dog's focus to be recalled. "That will do," says that a task underway has been pursued and now it is time to leave it—shift gears off of that task and bring your focus back here, and be at ease.

On another note, I do not let my horses graze in a bridle, side pull, or halter. When such tack is on their heads it means we have work to do and it is not time to side-track the mind and think about grazing. And when I take this tack off of a horse's head and walk away, the horse knows that it is now fine to graze or do whatever she wants to do. Here with our dogs, there is a similar situation with leashes. If a dog gets a leash put on, it is understood that something important is about to take place and a different focus becomes evident in the dog. But at any point, with or without tack or leash, it is helpful if the relationship between the person and the horse or dog is such that they're fine with leaving other things they might be thinking about and hear the human.

It seems that there is no question that a dog has the capability to discern between being on or off a job. And from listening to Harry tell his story and discuss it, I also can tell that just because he said "school's out," that did not signal to the dogs in his care that anything goes. They certainly were expected to act in a reasonable manner even when on their own time. And that brings us back to my question from the beginning of this chapter—can the relationship with the human remain consistent when a dog is on or off the clock? There are quite varying opinions on this topic, but let me throw out my own thoughts on the matter.

Coming at this from horse experience, I say yes. I have seen many horses make changes for the better because of the work done in a "school's in" setting. Horses can develop an all around better feeling about a person even in the "school's out" time in the pasture, paddock, or barn. Horses can become more ready to come up to people when they are loose and be more relaxed and open to interactions with people and even other horses in general, for example.

Developing a willing relationship with a dog, it seems to me, requires a full-on commitment. Consistency seems critical to getting a dog trained well and feeling good about working with people. And while there may be jobs to do with dogs—fetch a lost fly mask, herd some stock, or do some tricks—I hope that building the regular relationship between us enhances both our "schools in" and "schools out" time together. That the very essence of the relationship permeates all the interactions between us, whether they be more of a job or more just hanging out.

Often when I teach horsemanship I talk about how horses are never off, that horses are learning from us all of the time. It is a common theme with handy horse people to realize that from the moment we are with a horse until we finish interacting with them and walk away they are learning from us, whether we realize it or not. And sometimes we teach them things by accident that we wish we hadn't.

It is common to see a horse look right past a person and crowd the human so that the person backs up. This situation results from the person teaching the horse that it is okay to not take the person into consideration when in close proximity. If people had an awareness that the horse was mentally elsewhere and pushing overtop of them then they might get more particular in that area so that they get the horse's focus and not get pushed around or stepped on. The same is true of leading a horse. People often walk along with a horse who has a head high in the air, calling out, and is anything but really in tune or in step with them. The more this goes on the more it becomes the established relationship and a habit where keeping in touch with the human is not much of a priority to the horse.

Ellie Mae, being a German Shepherd/Belgian Malinois cross, had a powerful work drive and a busy mind. When she was younger, I had a real job keeping her from running off after deer. I would have loved to have had a working recall with her at that time, but I did not get that set up well early on and off she'd go if she came across deer at much of a distance from me. If she was close, it seemed as though my sphere of influence held up better. I needed to have had it better set up with her to let go of thoughts in general. In retrospect, I did not have that working nearly well enough in close quarters and even on leash to get it working at much of a distance. At this point in my life, with Ellie Mae now gone many months, I am searching for my next dog—a Border Collie puppy. I have plans to get the relationship between us more solid from the outset than I did with Ellie Mae.

The bottom line is that in general, if handled right over

time, a dog can let go of other things and be available to do whatever a person might ask, whenever the person might ask it. And the dog can feel good and relaxed about being with a human when doing tasks. If the best place in the world for my dog is being with me, then it hardly gets better than that. And I believe that a willingness can build as part of such a relationship across all that we do together.

Chapter Nine
Calmness vs. Excitement

A huge curiosity of mine is considering the canine state of mind and the way that it effects dogs and their relationships to humans. Specifically, I have been pondering the difference between dogs' minds being excited or calm, and all that flows from these two conditions.

I've mentioned how excited a dog can get when a person comes home from being away for some amount of time, like being at work. The "waggle factor" shows up here as the dog is thrilled to see the owner. I also mentioned herding dogs who get over-excited and grip sheep. These excitements are rooted in what we might consider to be positive scenarios. The dog's mind becomes excited because of being exuberant about thoughts that he "loves." I might add to this list other examples we've discussed so far like Gladys with her crazed state when playing with toys and Titus's seeing a person enter the kennel and knowing that he is about to get let outside.

Then, there are catalysts that excite the canine mind that we consider to be negative. Fear and worry are big ones, and if you have been around rescues much, you likely have seen a dog's mind excited by fear along the lines of what Kona showed, cowering and avoiding, and clearly stressed out. Sometimes that shows up as aggression with growling or posturing, or even biting. These behaviors clearly are the result of negative stress in the dog's mind and they kick in the self preservation instincts.

The point of listing these things that excite dogs' minds is that I have come to think of all of them, both positive and negative, as being in the way of a dog having a calm and, one might say, "sober" mind. If the canine mind is not sober, then it is not fully available to be with the human in a connected way. It also is observable that the dog is stressing. Even if we might spin that stress as positive or negative, the fact remains that the dog's mind is not at ease and this also shapes behavior and stirs up a variety of physical reactions.

For instance, it is pretty obvious that if a dog is dubious of a person and shying away from him or her that such a condition impacts the relationship. If a person asks something of a dog in this state of mind—like to sit—the dog is not fully present (all in) with the person to accomplish that request. The fear is in the way of the dog performing his best with and for the person.

But this same thing can be said about a dog who becomes very excited when we return home and walk in the door or pick up a leash to go for a walk. That exuberance overwhelms some of the ability of the dog's mind to focus, relax, and hear what the person may ask.

So, while there is no question that I would want to get rid of any negative reactions in a dog, what about the "positive" ones? I have been wondering if it is okay for a dog to get an excited mind over things that he loves? And, I have wondered about whether a dog might be okay to get into such a state during "school's out" time even if I were to block it during "school's in" time?

Another point to consider is that the positively excited mind does not produce a particularly good feeling in a dog. It can get to be more like a runaway train or a car with no brakes. It is a somewhat manic mindset. If you have ever felt frenzied with too much to do in too short of a time frame to accomplish it—even if it is all great stuff to cram into the afternoon like a birthday party, picking up a package of something you really want from the Post Office, grabbing a pizza, etc.—then you get the idea. If left to snowball, in dogs this zeal can end up in some pretty bad behaviors, or even, as we say in the horse world, a wreck (like being knocked down by a dog or some similar bigger physical calamity). One question this brings up for me is if the dog is able to let such a mindset go if asked to?

When working with horses, there are times when their attention gets drawn away from a person. The horsemanship that I practice and teach is centered on centering the horse's thoughts with the person in the moment. This is how one is able to get a change in a horse and help a horse to relax. But, we are in the real world. Other horses come into view, dogs bark close by, and all kinds of distractions can be present. I am not seeking a relationship with my horse where the horse stands at military attention and never considers looking away from me. As Harry points out, "That would make for a pretty funny looking ride!"

Rather, if something in the environment is of interest or concern, I want my horse to recognize it and maybe even have a look. But—and this is a really big but—if I ask my horse to let it go, she immediately should be able to disengage mentally from that distraction and be available to come back to me and hear what I have to say next. This is the same kind of idea that comes to mind when I think of dogs becoming wound up with positive stimuli.

Take for example a dog who gets excited when her owner gets a leash. The dog loves to go walking and has been allowed to get all revved up when the leash comes into view and starts jumping around and spinning circles. Is the owner able to speak to the dog and have her let go of that over-excitement, calm down, and sit or stand attentively? Or is the dog not able to hear the human so that the bouncing around continues? And a dog who is not able to let go of the thoughts that send her into a tizzy fit will be stuck experiencing the physical stressors that accompany that mindset, much like a dog would if it was in fear or in a panic.

Taking from horsemanship, I think about Titus and the kennel excitement he showed at first. There, I slapped my leg and stomped the floor to get the little terrier to let go of all that eager bouncing around and look me up. Jack Knox says, get a correction working; give the dog freedom to do whatever, and then correct the wrongs but don't try to make the right. I can see my work with Titus as a correction. And I did not tell Titus to sit or calm down, but rather I just corrected him when he was bonkers and then went on with the business at hand as if I expected him to follow along. And he did, until he didn't again, and then I corrected him again and we got back on track.

I am finding that this is the key to many problems that I have come across with dogs. Get big enough in some way to be important in their world. Then provide a great connection between you and the dog to be the basis of the relationship. It sounds easy when put that way. And sometimes it really is that easy. But then again, depending on the dog and what baggage from previous human relationships or other challenges that might be following a dog around, it may not be so easy.

Regardless of the challenges that a dog presents, I am convinced that a dog's mental focus is essential for a more relaxed and harmonious relationship with a human, and this is certainly the same with horses. Much of dogmanship, then, becomes a question of how to develop a relationship with a dog that brings their interactions in tune with ours with a willing submission to our requests? One ingredient, I've discovered, is working to have a sober dog. Any excitement that tips the dog from a calm mind to a frenzied, agitated, or manic mind is in the way of a happy dog and a good relationship with the handler. I'm not talking about some happy tail wagging or trotting up to see a person, but I am referring to any amped-up state of mind. And people can be pretty bad about revving up that mental excitedness mistaking it for happiness or love from a dog. Even praise for something that we are looking for, like the completion of a trick, can excite the dog's mind too far and get in the way.

However, I do find that praise can be very helpful when handled thoughtfully and in the right doses for an individual dog. If we take a Border Collie who loves herding above all else in life, or a retriever who likewise is hard wired to love retrieving, those dogs have a built in reward for accomplishing those tasks. It is easy to see a capable Border Collie hit the sweet spot when working sheep. The herding dog needs no praise to improve on the reward of working stock, and praise may well even detract from the fulfillment of that task. But what about other kinds of dogs, like the rescue mutt who has who-knows-what breeds in him and none of them has any kind of work ethic? How is such a dog motivated?

Well, one glimpse at YouTube videos is all it takes to realize that people tend to use food treats ad nauseum to accomplish this in a huge number of cases. Now, before everyone goes burning me at the stake for my fairly anti-food treat stance, let me first say that I am not against all use of food treats. However, in general, I think of treats this way—that instead of there being two entities in the relationship that we are working on, the dog and the person, now we have three, the dog, the person, and the TREAT. And the treat can be a whole lot more attention grabbing than the person.

I am just too selfish to want to share my dog with another, especially more enticing and inanimate, thing. I want my dog to want to be with me, not the treat that I am holding in my hand or that is in my pocket. But I will admit, that even I have used treats in certain circumstances. The big one that comes to mind is when teaching a dog to roll over. I never gave Ellie Mae food treats. But when I went to teach her to roll over when she was about eight years old, I had to figure out some way to help her to get the idea. I got her to lie down on one side, and then I used a piece of cracker to attract her attention. Then I led her nose with the cracker to get her to roll over and switch sides, and then I praised her. After two of those with crackers, she had it and I did not go back to using the treat again.

And, I praised her when she got each roll over completed. And that praise did become what she sought in the trick. I am not a hundred percent sure how I feel about the praising with her, even though it worked and it seemed not to go over board. Again, how does one encourage a pet who has no drive for a given task? It seems that a bit of praise may be the best choice. But even then, can the handler not over-excite the dog's mind. Can the handler end the praise and have the dog's attention back? Or does the praise cause a problem and thus a separation in the dog/human relationship?

It's pretty clear to see that I am asking as many questions as I am answering here. And to make matters more complex, each dog and situation is different. So even if I am able to spell out just the right recipe for Ellie Mae, that's not going to fit for Rover or Spot or Bocephus.

But, these kinds of questions really get me digging around to find some answers. Another Ellie Mae example comes to mind.

When Ellie Mae was a pup, I had it in mind to get her earning her keep around here by finding and fetching lost fly masks in the horse pastures. This is a really big help. But, I soon discovered that Ellie Mae had not one ounce of retrieving instinct in her. Zero.

To begin this fly mask fetching scheme of mine, I began by just randomly placing a fly mask so that when we were together, she would happen to come across it. Her natural curiosity made that an easy task. I would hide one inside the house or in the yard. Then, when she found it and went to sniffing it, I would praise her pretty hard and say, "Good fly mask! Good fly mask!" It did not take long before a fly mask was the greatest thing on earth, just by praising her for coming across one. Soon, by using a long rope attached to her collar, I would place a fly mask in view at some distance, have her sitting or lying down by me, and then say "Ellie Mae, fly mask," and she would go to it and then I would draw her back to me and have her drop it at my feet, and I praised her.

Ellie Mae possessed a super mind and this all went well. Soon she was able to fetch a fly masks at liberty without needing to be reminded to bring it to me with the long line. Then, we graduated to the pasture. I was able for the entirety of her adult life to take her to a fence or gate, send her on a mission by saying "Ellie Mae, fly mask," and off she would go looking for a fly mask. When she found one, she would grab it up and lift it the best she could, dragging it along to one side of her, return to me with it, and drop it at me feet. The fly mask fetch was one of our greatest accomplishments.

Several lessons really stick with me from training Ellie Mae on the fly mask fetching task. First was that praise was an effective and powerful tool to get it working. And the beauty of praise (especially over giving a treat) is that the praise comes from me (is part of me) and is a function of the relationship. She was looking to me and interested in doing her part in the relationship and making me happy. This is different from a conditioned response where the dog performs some task and gets some other thing or avoids some specific negative experience. I think of a conditioned response as being a rather mechanical exchange, for lack of a better word, as opposed to a task mutually accomplished with a living feel between a person and a dog, or horse for that matter.

It brings me back to the main theme of this book, which is my quest to build the best possible, willing relationship between a dog and a person. Praise, I think, in dogs—especially dogs who lack a natural instinct to accomplish certain tasks—is a great tool if used judiciously. But, over-do it, and dogs get revved up and begin to loose their mindfulness, and that starts to become a hindrance to a relaxed and attentive dog and gets in the way of the relationship.

Chapter Ten
Straightness

Straightness or crookedness in a horse's body when performing tasks is a big-time indicator of where the horse's mind is or is not focused. This is true in both leading or riding a horse. If a horse is thinking forward to a place that I also would like to go—imagine riding to a water trough across a pasture, for example—then the horse is operating in a way to take himself to that place. Every part of his body and my body will be operating to take us there, and the rider can feel the whole of the horse's body being straight in the task.

Perhaps more important is what the rider does not feel. Namely, that there is no resistance or side-tracking going on within the horse that spills over into a cattywompus crookedness as the horse goes along. There is a real togetherness, and one might say that it simply weighs nothing between the person and the horse.

By contrast, if the person has in mind to direct a horse to that water trough but the horse's mind is off in another direction on some distraction, like going back to the barn, then the horse's body reflects that distracted desire. It becomes palpable that the horse is pulling away in some ways even as the rider attempts to manipulate the horse to go the way he wants to go. I find the same kind of thing to be true when working with dogs.

When I was working a lot with different rescue dogs, I did a bunch of walking dogs around on leashes. Every so often I would come across one who either was well leash trained or who had a natural desire to follow along with me with just a little work. These dogs were a joy to direct because they fell in place where I wanted them to. That might be, for instance, in the sweet spot to my side and a little behind me when walking along with them. It weighed nothing between us to go along together. And the difference between a dog thinking along with me on a leash or not is every bit as obvious as a horse who is crooked when being ridden or led with a mind not centered and going with what the person presents.

My son Cody Moates is a professional dog trainer in Charlotte, North Carolina. He's been a certified master dog trainer for over a couple of decades now. When we get together, I enjoy comparing notes on similarities and differences between working with dogs and horses. Cody is the only dog trainer that I have heard mention straightness in dogs.

Not long ago, my wife Carol adopted a rescue puppy named Victor. Victor came to her as the runt of a litter who at first was about the size of a mouse, some four pounds less than his robust siblings, and was not expected to live. Victor needed to be bottle fed and remarkably he persevered and gained strength and size and now at a year old is a solid 75 pounds. The blue coated mutt has ended up with some issues, though. One being that he is not well balanced in his body. Victor kind of wobbles when he walks. He gets around okay, but I have described his motility challenge by saying that his internal gyroscope is off.

Cody was around Victor early on as we were trying to get him leading on a leash. Cody said, "Get him to follow and get straight and not be dragging you around on a leash." Victor makes this a particularly interesting statement because he never is really straight in his walking. And yet, he is an excellent example of a dog getting straight in the other sense of being led that Cody was talking about.

Victor, even with a wobbly gait, is fully capable of falling in line with a person on the leash when walking. He can hit the sweet spot at times as well as any dog I have worked with. Even with his gyroscopic challenges, when his mind is with me and he is walking along on leash, he weighs nothing and there is slack in the leash.

Victor's condition is a great opportunity for me to feel that straightness has everything to do with leading a dog's willing mind and not really about manipulating the dog's body. Yes, a dog's body may be straight-ish when he is thinking along with a person, although many dogs track with the hind end off to one side pretty much all of the time and are really not straight per se. But the straightness I mean here is easily felt when leading Victor even though he is not mechanically capable of really going anything resembling straight within his body.

I was very taken by Cody using the word straight when talking about leading a dog. I wondered why I had not come across other dog trainers using the term in this way. And I discussed his use of the term and what he meant by it in more detail.

Cody said that he really had not meant straightness in the dog's body the way that I apply it in some instances to horses. But he did mean it just as his above quote says: "Get him to follow and get straight and not be dragging you around on a leash." Cody is saying, get this situation straightened out and do not be dragged around on the leash. And Cody added more thoughts that I enjoyed considering.

"I don't want to lead the dog," Cody explained.

That statement was a head-scratcher at first. Of course we want to lead our dogs around, right? But then he followed that up by saying, "I want the dog paying attention to me."

Aha! This relates to my horsemanship bang-on. I do not want a horse pulling on me or dragging me around or stepping on me. I am going to get big enough with a horse to get the horse's mind centered up with me and be directable. And then wherever I go, the idea is to get the horse to follow along with slack in the lead rope, or even at liberty. The same is true for dogs and leashes. And there were additional similarities that I was able to relate to horsemanship.

"The leash only gets tight when the dog is distracted," Cody continued. "A squirrel, a guy on a bicycle, and you're no longer number one on his mind."

Yes! That's what I'm talking about.

"It's not a tow strap," Cody said.

That was all music to my ears. And because of my horse work, I was easily able to follow what he meant. It was exactly what I had been discovering worked with dogs, as I discussed in a previous chapter regarding Titus, for example.

I think one reason that the term straightness gets used much more by horse people than by dog people is because horses get ridden. Being atop a horse and going along, it becomes more obvious if the animal is crooked than when we do not ride the creature. And even horse people who are clueless about the influence of a horse's mind on straightness often recognize crookedness in a mechanical sense and will work to bring about

Here I am leading Carol's rescue dog Victor. He's tracking along very nicely on the slack leash in the sweet spot, just behind me, following the feel I present. (Photo: Carol Moates)

straightness in a horse by mechanical means. People will use legs, spurs, and reins to push and pull the horse's body into position even if they ignore that the horse is distracted and that the side-tracked mind is the root of the crookedness.

Cody has worked many hundreds more dogs than I likely

ever will. And having a conversation that showed me that he has become aware of when they hit the sweet spot when being led and that he is keen to see people get that straight was an important insight for me. It said to me that even if Cody doesn't use quite the same vocabulary when discussing dog training as I do when talking about horsemanship, there can be words and ideas that do overlap. One does not get straightness in a horse over any length of time unless the horse's mind is available to be directed by the person. I now find it safe to say the same is true when discussing the relationship between dogs and humans, too.

Chapter Eleven
Observation

Of all the beneficial traits that a person can possess to help figure out how to build better relationships between dogs (and horses) and us humans, there is one that really jumps out at me: observation.

Getting to spend a great deal of time with Harry Whitney over nearly two decades now has been a huge blessing in many ways, including improving my horsemanship, to say the least. But where did Harry acquire these remarkable skills he has with horses? Did the gift come naturally or did Harry learn from someone else?

Harry gets asked this from time-to-time at clinics. I have heard him answer on numerous occasions that he did not have a mentor. And that by his teenage years, he was well on the way towards putting together in his mind and in practice what has become his unique approach to horsemanship that focuses on horses' thoughts.

As a long time student and friend of Harry's, I have my

own theory on this. I am convinced that Harry has an uncanny ability to observe at a level higher than a great many people do. I think that Harry must have been born with this aptitude, although surely there must be some environmental influences at work, as well. But the point here is that for whatever reason, Harry sees the whole horse—or dog, for that matter—with nuances of depth that allow him to address many spots to help relieve these animals' anxieties and get them more mentally with a person that others simply do not recognize.

Many people know that Harry is an accomplished photographer. For some years, prints of his photos were available for sale and sold extensively. His photos ran in magazines, and he has won at least one distinguished award from a national magazine for his photos. There is no doubt in my mind that Harry's high level of observational ability is likewise why he is such an impressive photographer. Harry sees so much, but when I think about it it fascinates me that, really, Harry only can see what is there to be seen. And if something is there to be seen, then it is there to be seen by anybody, right? Once he points out some aspect of a horse, or some other thing, perhaps even something in a person's life, for example, people react, "Oh yeah...you're right! Look at that!"

Without seeing subtle expressions, movements, intentions, and so forth—a look in the eye, respiration rates or holding of the breath, tail position, how the legs move and the feet land, ear position, and on and on—people miss how a dog or horse is feeling. And certainly, therefore, they miss any chance or idea of how to intervene to help resolve some issue when it is a small thing before it gets going and becomes an established undesirable behavior.

I talked earlier about how humans must work on things with dogs and horses in the moment. But the thing is, issues present in moments often long before many people observe and register any sign of them. Humans may miss the chance to nip an issue in the bud with a dog or horse when it is more easily cleared out. If we can be observant, we may see tension and worry in little particular areas like a look in the eye or swish of the tail and intervene before the dog ever barks or the horse ever bucks.

This high level of observation I also attribute to Jack Knox when working with Border Collies. Jack sees things in those dogs that others, including the owners, just do not typically see. Jack points them out in the hope that others will see them and that the new awareness will get things going better between the dogs and the people...and the sheep.

Another thing about Harry and Jack, and probably any gifted hand, is that I am sure that it is a mystery to them how others do not see these things. And how people do not see them happening well before the dog is running amuck all over a field or a horse is stepping on their feet.

I often have shared one of Harry's recurring quotes in my horsemanship books and in horsemanship lessons that is fitting here: "Until you see it, you don't see it; and then when you do see it, you wonder how you never saw THAT before!" And I will take the liberty to tack onto that: "And now you can't unsee it."

Some of the progress in my horsemanship resulted from A-HA! moments that Harry's teaching brought on. Some of it I learned from the horses themselves. And some of it was a slow culmination of understanding that occurred over time from a range of different influences with Harry's teaching clearly being the foundation of how I think and go about it. But all of it resulted from my improved ability to observe the horses or dogs in front of me, feel of them, soak in the moment, truly see what is in right front of my face, and then try something fitting to the situation to get a positive change in the critter. The horses and dogs definitely let you know if your approach works, or not, in any given instance.

And it is worth a mention here that there are tough cases that have Harry and Jack challenged, too. I have witnessed this with both of them in clinics. There are horses and dogs that have kept them up at night wondering how to get a positive change going. I find it inspiring in a way, that no matter how much a person knows, how observant a person is, or how experienced a trainer is, that there always is more to learn.

Horses and dogs can teach us plenty. I have come to see how in our interactions with dogs and horses that really, it is we humans who change what we do in order to bring about change in the relationships with these animals. The dogs and horses are in the moment, but are we? And what is there to truly see in the moment to help guide us in how we approach the animals? I have seen plenty of tears shed at clinics over the years—tears of frustration, joy, and realization. I am convinced that people who make progress with getting their animals feeling better and who develop a more positive and willing relationship with them have achieved that by breaking new ground within themselves. And that can be quite a moving experience.

Shifts in people and how they approach their dogs or horses is really what changes things up for the animals in the situation. It is a new understanding in the humans that leads to a change in how things feel between both the people and the critters, and that leads to a change of behavior, too. And we achieve the first step of that process by altering our understanding of situations. A huge part of getting to that point is accomplished through observation.

If we can see what's going on, then we can mull it over in our minds. If we can not perceive it, then we do not even know it exists to be dealt with. And living in a world of massive distractions as a way of life (don't even get me started on smart phones in front of faces every waking moment), it can require a seismic shift in a person's very way of life and habits to get to the point of meeting our dogs and horses where they are to help them and build a different kind of relationship with them. But it can happen, and in really exciting ways. I know it can; I have observed it many times.

Carol and her beloved dog Zeke, a Giant Schnauzer/Bullmastiff cross, at our home in Floyd, Virginia. (Photo: Christian Marsh)

Chapter Twelve
Working with Ellie Mae

One of my high hopes right from Ellie Mae's puppyhood was that eventually she would be able to tag along with me as I rode horses around the farm and on trails. The prospect proved challenging as she got old enough for me to consider working on it. The big thing was that when I was horseback, I needed her to follow commands at a distance. Even though she had gotten the swing of "sit" and "lie down" very quickly, the only way she accomplished those requests was to trot over to me and perform them right at my feet.

When I attempted the conversation to get her to stay at a distance from me and sit or lie down, there seemed to be no getting the point across. Ellie Mae might be 10 feet away from me, for example, and I'd say, "sit!" She immediately would approach me and only then sit right by my feet. Great sit; lousy timing with her side-track to draw to me first.

A bit belatedly came the flash of realization that I was at least partly to blame for this problem. I had worked on these two commands with Ellie Mae for some months. Now I wondered, could it be that I was calling her to me to do them? Hmmmm. Or, at the very least, I certainly had been oblivious to falling into the trap of having her approach me each time she performed them. Her great sits and lie downs had so pleased me that I had simultaneously and generously rewarded both the wanted and unwanted behaviors going on. Now, I was kicking myself for building in a conditioned response to have her first come to me when performing them.

By now, Ellie Mae had some size on her. It was time to start working with her from horseback and the coming-in-close issue jumped out at me. The first thing I tried to do to fix it was to just block her coming all the way to me after I spoke a command. The plan was to get her to sit or lie down at a small distance away from me. Then I would incrementally get her to perform those tasks farther away from me until it was working at any distance. I was thinking about Harry's line about horses, "It's amazing what they won't do if you don't let them."

Apparently, that ship had sailed. This approach seemed useless to get her to sit or lie down at even a short distance from me. She pushed in anyway or, if I got really persistent, she would leave the scene. I surely did not want her to begin ignoring my commands altogether or taking them as a reason to go off away from me in avoidance. Perhaps this would have gone better if I had been blocking her advancing towards me, at least some of the time, when I gave the commands at the very beginning of her training to sit and lie down. Or perhaps Ellie was just a brutally tough case?

Lamenting over my difficulties and ruminating over what to try next, I spoke to Harry about the problem. Harry suggested getting a long rope attached to Ellie's collar and then running the rope around a post or a tree so that I could exercise better control over her distance from me. Perhaps then I could work on getting her to sit and lie down and not allow the unwanted behavior.

In retrospect, this approach seems pretty simple. To me at the time, though, it seemed more like true genius! A shift in the human's thought process spurred by using ingenuity often is the doorway to a horse or dog trainer's positive results. And I had been having trouble sparking my thinker to come up with a solution to try outside of standing there and working on it at liberty.

So I got my 40 foot lariat, undid the loop, and attached the brass metal ring it has for a honda to Ellie Mae's collar with a clip. Next, I arranged it around a stump so that Ellie Mae faced me and the rope went behind her, around the stump, and back past her to my hand. The stump acted like a pulley so that I was able to dial Ellie Mae to various distances from me. This method worked very well. Her strong draw to me when I gave the commands meant that she pulled against the tight rope running behind her to the stump. This slowed down her response of moving her feet to the point that she was able to hear and process the commands to sit or lie down while being away from me. It took some shuffling, but with some patience and letting her work out what I was looking for—closer to me at first and then increasing the space between us—she got on board with the idea rather quickly.

We worked on this each day for about a week until I was getting easy responses to the commands up to about 30 feet away from me. At this point, the slack was not coming out of the rope when I gave the commands; she just performed them. Then came the moment of truth—trying it without the rope. Starting quite close at first, I asked Ellie to sit and boom! She sat right there when I asked. Farther away proved a little more iffy. Out about 20 feet or more I blocked her pretty hard by putting up a hand and saying "aught!" to avoid her advancing a few steps. I went back to using the rope a bit more to tune that up better at a distance. Soon, I was really happy with the results and even without the rope Ellie Mae had the idea. And for the rest of Ellie Mae's life, getting her to sit or lie down at a distance was never a problem.

Like with horses, sometimes putting in a bit of time to clear up a problem is well worth it and makes for many years of more enjoyable interactions.

At this point, I got to thinking about getting Ellie Mae out on the trail with me when I was horseback. I wondered if she would act differently if I climbed up on a horse as opposed to standing on the ground when I gave commands? This came to mind in part because time and again I have seen horses doing well in the ground work with people standing on the ground but get the person to stand on a mounting block or sit on a fence and the whole thing falls apart. I put Ellie Mae in the round pen and I climbed up and sat atop a panel. When I asked Ellie to sit, it was interesting that my being up on the panel did indeed confuse her. She sat, but only by reverting to the former behavior of coming over close to me and then sitting by the bottom of the panel.

It was necessary to get the lariat out again and run it around a pipe in the panels across the round pen from where I sat and clip it to her collar. With a very small effort this time, I was able to get Ellie Mae to sit and lie down at various distances on request with the aid of the rope just as I had managed when standing on the ground and using the stump as a pulley outside of the round pen. The lesson had sunk in, but the presentation of my being up on the fence had to be related to it. It was not hard to get working, and so next came the real test...to see if Ellie Mae could hear me and follow my direction when I was in the saddle.

I tacked up Carol's gelding Niji and mounted. Ellie Mae was loose in the yard where I sat atop the horse. Ellie Mae was puttering around sniffing the ground and tending to dog things about 15 feet away.

"Sit!" I said.

She immediately sat and looked up at me. What a triumphant moment that was!

"Lie down," I continued.

She happily eased herself all the way down to the ground.

"Okay!" I released her.

Up she stood and went sauntering off a ways with her petticoats swishing side-to-side to begin sniffing around a grape arbor.

Yes! The work paid off.

Over time, I got a quite a few additional lines of communication opened with Ellie Mae. When I would say, "go git!" she would take off and go on ahead of me. I could point in a direction when I said it, and she would go in that direction. Another helpful deal was that if we were going along walking together (or if I was horseback) and Ellie Mae was out ahead of me, I could give one quick whistle and she would check in with me. If you are a horse person, think half-halt. She would not quit moving forward, but she would turn her head, slow down slightly, and soften a bit, seeing if there was anything else I would ask of her. And as with a half-halt, often that is all I was looking for—just to see if she was indeed there with me mentally and available in

Ellie Mae and me down at the river on our place.

case I did want to ask anything else of her.

If I gave two quick whistles together, she would stop moving and check in with me. This was a more serious "quit going and really look at me" request. She was able to do these whistle responses even at large distances from me. Next, I could release her back to her own doings by saying "okay" or in a specific direction by saying "go git." And being able to have Ellie Mae that steerable from the ground and from the saddle was both great fun and helpful when there arose certain circumstances like critters drawing her attention or my wanting to get her in a definite safe spot if, for example, a vehicle was coming up the road.

Later on, I discovered an interesting benefit to having her along with me when trail riding my mare, Mirage. Sometimes Mirage could be pretty on edge when we would go riding around on the trails on our land. We have Black Bear, deer, turkeys, and a whole host of other wild creatures that live here or come through at times, so her fears certainly are founded in that regard. At times when Mirage was on higher alert, if I brought Ellie Mae with us, the mare was much more at ease. The horse knew that the dog had better sense and more capable senses than I do. And Mirage seemed to trust that dog not to miss anything potentially dangerous. So Mirage could watch the dog and not have to be in charge of being on guard for everything in the environment herself. If I sent Ellie Mae out in front of us, it was palpable how Mirage let down to a large extent, and I found that to be a really fun and helpful byproduct of the relationship I was building with Ellie Mae. And how great it was for a dog like Ellie Mae, who was bred to work, to have many jobs to perform with me.

As with horses, having a job to do with your dog provides things for you to do together, but this also is a good way to discover where you have things in the relationship working or not. Just like my struggling to get Ellie Mae to sit and lie down at a distance from me. It took me thinking about the "job" of having the dog go along with me when I was horseback to realize that she was on auto-pilot with that drawing to me first business. And what a huge bunch of opportunities opened up for us when we got that working.

That relationship where a dog is really keeping you in mind and is willing to follow what you ask her to do is one of the most sublime feelings I know. Again, as with horses, there is just something about not only getting a communication going with another species, but such a connection and relationship established that the critter is able to be at ease and a willing partner. It is truly amazing, and I am forever striving to get more of it working in my dogmanship and horsemanship.

Chapter Thirteen
Leading

Getting a dog leading well, as with horses, helps with more than just getting the dog from point A to point B. It goes a long way towards developing a relationship in which a dog is generally stable and willing to follow a human's direction. In the range of dogs that I have worked with in rescues and elsewhere, I have found that both waiting (like at the kennel door for a dog to settle down and think) and getting assertive with some intervention (like saying "Hey!" or slapping my leg) can help get a dog's mind centered and calmer. There is no one-option-fits-all approach since each dog is different, so keeping a range of options at the ready is important for success. But as discussed previously, getting canines' minds focused is essential to communicating with them—if they are tuning you out mentally, no real communication is going to take place. At the very least, getting the dog focused there on you is a starting point for a conversation.

Once a person gets a dog's focus truly centered up with him or her, it is time to do something with that attention. The intent is that the person now can direct that attention so that the dog's actions follow along with what the person has in mind for the dog to do—a trick, herd sheep, or maybe just follow you along on a slack leash.

The hope is to work towards interactions between the person and a dog that are calm and willing. As I think about this part of the dog/human connection, I circle back to my curiosity about the pack dynamic. How is it that dogs can view humans in such a way as to submit willingly to our direction when being led on a leash or otherwise?

As Harry often explains at clinics, all horses come into the world ready to follow a capable leader. It seems canines also come into the world hard-wired to submit to a capable leader. What constitutes a capable leader from one dog to the next is a moving target, but I think that the general idea holds true. It is this instinctual trait in dogs to follow a pack leader that humans are able to capitalize on. Being able to lead a dog isn't something that people invented on their own (although we did invent the leash). Instead, we borrow the potential for that kind of relationship from the dogs themselves. So what goes into a person becoming a leader in a pack, even if that is just a pack of two?

Recently at the local library, I perused the dog book section and checked out Caesar Millan's Short Guide to a Happy Dog. Caesar is a well known TV personality who trains dogs and has a reputation for successful outcomes. Perhaps I should mention that I only have seen a handful of videos of Caesar working with dogs. But from what I have seen, he seems very handy. I was especially curious to know what he might have to say about pack dynamic.

Getting down to the nitty-gritty, Caesar says in this book, "Everything comes back to these four words: 'be the pack leader.'"

Well, that's a pretty definitive statement coming from an

accomplished dog trainer like Caesar. Most problems people have with dogs, according to Caesar, come directly from the lack of adequate pack leadership from the human. And another point Caesar makes is that the work one does with dogs to get established as pack leader should be to bring a dog to a condition of "calm, submissive energy."

See...easy, right?

A photo of Caesar accompanies this section of the book showing him walking a pack of at least 20 loose dogs of all different kinds. As he walks confidently along, the entire pack trails him, each one looking relaxed and following willingly. If a picture can convey a person who has the pack leader role figured out and working, this one does just that. It is very impressive.

It also reasserted my finding that it is best for the human to be out front when walking a dog, on a leash or at liberty. It is so interesting that most dogs I see being walked on a leash are out in front of their humans. Trailing behind seems to be the human default position with dogs. I bet everyone reading this book has witnessed plenty of cases where it came to mind, "Look, that dog is walking the person!" You know, those instances where the dog truly drags the person along wherever the canine wants to go. I have to wonder why, if people want to be the ones leading, doesn't the idea of being out in front of dogs occur organically to humans? It is the very same situation with people and horses. And I, too, was plenty guilty of this until I began to have conversations and really start to get it sorted out, with horses first and then dogs later.

Another lesson I learned from working with horses is that whoever is out front in the leading process is taking in the world ahead visually. And with horses, as Harry often explains, almost always a horse's primary thought is the one that the horse's eyes are on. The same seems to be true with dogs. The one who is ahead in the leading deal, horse or hound, may not really be able see the person who is behind. Talk about assuming the lead role and relegating the person to a secondary thought. The one out front is directing the deal like a person driving a motorcycle with a the passengers who is behind, hanging on and just along for the ride.

This leads back to the notion that little things become big things with horses and dogs. If the person misses the point when a dog takes over the lead role in a small way, then the person may be surprised when "suddenly" the dog takes off and does something bigger and undesirable and the handler is unable to stop him. Being particular in how the situation is set up when walking a dog, going through a door with a dog, and even how we prepare a dog when we go to put a collar on the dog...all such things may have a lot of meaning to the dog in relation to who is in charge and who is following. The human may not even realize just how much such messages are being conveyed constantly to a dog.

This is a moment when the differences between humans and dogs really seems apparent to me. Dogs are forever assessing who is the leader and who isn't. This is super important to them and their safety. If the leader is faltering and no longer is viewed as a capable leader, for example, then it may be time for a follower dog to take care of number one and start doing the leading in the relationship. Humans, on the other hand, often seem to just want to go about life with dogs without thinking about such things. And, they want their dogs to like them. This combination can get people into trouble when it causes a lack of assertiveness and boundaries with dogs.

It is interesting to see that when people try to be super nice to their dogs to the point of letting the dogs run the show and run amuk that the dogs often become more worried and

Carol's rescue pup Glory follows along very nicely with me. She's traveling where I want her to be, a bit behind me and off to my left side, on a slack leash. (Photo: Carol Moates)

tense and show undesirable behaviors. It was for good reasons that Caesar said, "Everything comes back to these four words: 'be the pack leader.'" Experiencing a leadership role from the human helps bring about clarity in how the relationship is going to work. It helps the canine's mind to be centered, available, and thoughtful. As with horses, clarity provides structure and confidence and allows for relaxation and "calm, submissive energy" to use Caesar's words. Lack of a capable leader in the human leaves a lot of question marks in the dog's mind. This, in turn, can be a real problem in the human environment. If you've ever had a leather couch eaten or had food disappear from the counter, you know what I am talking about. Let alone more aggressive behaviors showing up in a dog that can be very troubling indeed. And leading a dog on a leash is such a great window into this realm of relationship and also is a way to help establish a leadership role with a dog.

Having a dog leading well may not necessarily spill over into all the other areas of your interactions together and improve those—although I believe that it has the potential to. But, there is no doubt that if a person can not lead a dog along on a slack leash with the dog following calmly behind the person, then the person clearly is not in the pack leader role and there are problems that need to be sorted out.

Chapter Fourteen
Nuances of Training

Sometimes with horse training, two varied approaches may seem similar to an unfamiliar onlooker. But if one is observant to the nuances of timing and feel, the two situations can be seen as really quite different. So, is this similar with regard to dog training? To give an example of what I mean, let's take flagging a horse in a round pen.

Many people teach a kind of horsemanship that advocates running a horse around in a round pen. The person heaps on the pressure so that when the person quits the pressure, that draws the horse into a vacuum in the middle of the pen to be in close proximity to the human. The horse usually is pretty quick to take the offer to come in and stand by the person to get a break. Typically, even though the horse comes quickly to the person, the horse harbors an ill feeling towards the person (the horse knows the person was driving him around). The horse often stands there with ears pinned, head high, and tail swishing with anxiety and a dubious feeling towards the person. But, even standing there upset is better to the average horse than being chased by a person around a corral.

By contrast, but perhaps seemingly similar, one can work with a horse in a round pen without driving the horse. The horse may begin by choosing to run around the pen. The non-driving person will tend to take up a position in the center of the pen, as do many of the horse-driving people. But notice that the non-driving person stands there quietly, simply offering that the horse stop all of that motion and come in and stand and be with the person quietly at any time.

These two presentations from the humans are polar opposites. But can the onlooker see the difference? This idea builds on an earlier chapter where the act of observing was discussed—can we see what is going on with the critters and people right in front of us?

When working with a horse in this kind of non-driving scenario, if the horse keeps up the running and is very distracted with his thoughts outside of the pen, the person may whack the flag against the ground. The intention of the whack is to draw the horse's mind back into the pen and towards the person. But at first, the whack may cause the horse to speed up. It may appear as though the horse was flagged to run faster even though that was not the case. The person may need to work at flagging occasionally, getting the horse to check the person out and bring the horse's mind into the pen bit-by-bit. And one amazing thing that often unfolds is that merely getting the horse to turn his attention back into the pen where his body is contained produces opportunities for the horse to feel better.

The horse's body runs around wildly wanting to get to where the horse's thoughts are—over outside of the pen. But only when the focus comes back into the pen and the horse's mind rejoins his body can the horse begin to take in his immediate surroundings and start to slow down, relax, and consider

Here's a photo I took of Harry in a round pen at a clinic in Stevensville, Montana. The horse is Sunshine, a mare owned by Linda Davenport. Sunshine's mind was outside of the pen and she was running wildly even as Harry stood quietly in the center of the pen. Harry is holding a stock whip, and with a series of well timed cracks, he was able to draw Sunshine's mind into the pen with him. Before too long, the mare chose to go to Harry and stand quietly with him.

truly being with the human. Many facets of this situation can be explained in greater detail, but that is the gist of it.

So, is this also true for dogs? Right away I think about Titus and how he was bouncing and barking in the kennel when we first met. It is a very common occurrence in rescue dog kennels and presents much like a horse who is upset and contained in a pen. The way I worked on things with Titus also involved an occasional noise-making on my part (slapping my leg or stomping my foot) that helped to get his mind more there in the kennel and with me in a similar way to round penning the horse described above.

What I did with Titus was quite different from what others had been doing. I later witnessed others walk into the kennel and there was Titus clambering and climbing the walls. They did not work or wait to get Titus to settle, but rather opened the kennel door during the midst of his raving behavior, did their best to catch the rascal, and muscled to hold him with one hand while attempting to place the slip lead onto his head with the other hand. As with the horse work mentioned above, these two approaches are vastly different in feel and approach and bring about very different results, but again may not look entirely different at first to the untrained eye.

Something else Cody said during one of our discussions stuck with me. It also sheds light onto the importance of getting a dog mentally centered when working on building the relationship and in the training.

"I don't do lessons at a dog park," Cody stated, simply.

I followed what he meant, but to be certain that I did, he added, "You're not going to give your kid homework to do at a circus."

In other words, when working on training a dog, the dog's focus is essential. Putting the dog in an environment with a ton of obviously strong distractions only works against that endeavor. I liked the dog park quote in particular because working a dog in a dog park might seem like an obvious place to give a dog lesson—that's where you take dogs and do things with them, after all, right?

But no, what could be more distracting to a dog than other dogs? Maybe rabbits and squirrels...but you get the idea. So if you want to get a child focused and doing homework then no...you are not going to take a child to the circus or the playground and ask him or her to work on homework there. The fact that Cody even brought this up proved to me that he had been down the road of mentioning it many times before, so people clearly miss this aspect of training at times.

The point really is that having dogs' minds present is essential to improving our relationships with them. Further into our conversation, Cody did say that if things progressed well with the training between the owner and a dog that later he may take the lessons over close to a dog park, but not in it. If the client is able to get that working really well with a dog, only then might Cody suggest taking the dog into the dog park.

And that's the hope, right? That we are able to develop the kind of relationship with our dogs that they would rather be together with us and following our lead, regardless of where we find ourselves, than in any other situation. That in any place and at any time, dogs are able to hear what we humans say to them and that they can let go of all the other distractions and focus on us when we ask something of them.

Certainly this kind of a relationship is needed if a herding dog is to herd stock with a person, if a police dog is to go after a bad guy in the heat of a battle at the behest of a handler, if a service dog is to guide a blind person along a busy street, or if a pet is to come and sit calmly by an owner when someone new comes in the door. Using a round pen to get a horse more with a person or a kennel to help a dog settle with a handler are good places to work on this kind of thing. Starting that training somewhere manageable really helps.

Safety and well being are better assured when we can communicate with our dogs and they are willing to hear what we say and act on what we ask of them. And the truth is, it also is a great deal more fun when our dogs listen to us and desire wholeheartedly to perform what we ask of them. And it often seems like a two-way street; that dogs also benefit from and enjoy such a relationship, one where they are able to feel relaxed, safe, and happy to be led by a capable leader.

To achieve that kind of directing role with a horse or a dog, we need to discern the difference between driving a horse around the round pen or drawing the horse to us, or, forcing a slip lead on an antsy dog at the kennel door or getting the dog's mind centered and calm so that it is easy to slip the lead over the calm dog's head with no ruckus. These differences are really differences in the kind of relationships we build with our critters through the way that we approach our work with them.

Chapter Fifteen

The Big Fork in the Road

Many similarities between working with horses and working with dogs have been highlighted in this book, and they are fun to focus on. But what about the opposite—those aspects of working with dogs that are markedly different from working with horses?

Reflecting on this questions, it is clear to me that there is one particularly massive difference between the two species. (Well, two if you count the fact that you can not usually bring your horse inside the house with you or have him jump up in the pickup and ride in the seat beside you.) And this is a difference that really defines a great deal of the behaviors with the two species. Horses are prey animals who graze for a living, and by large contrast, dogs are predators who are natural hunters. Thus, horses and dogs are at opposite ends of the food and lifestyle spectrum, and that seriously effects some of how they interact with others of their own species, with us humans, and with their environments.

First, I will admit that I think sometimes people get carried away with the horses being prey animals idea. Yes, at times people might be viewed by horses as predators (especially when we act like it!). But I have heard some rants about horses having trouble with people because we smell like the meat we eat, for example, and I just have not seen that kind of thing to be true. So, I do think there is something at play there but not enough to go overboard—too many really good relationships evolve between horses and carnivorous people to buy into some of that.

Second, I admit to not having much fear with a massive horse who is standing on hind legs posturing to take me out, but even a 15 pound mutt at my feet snarling at me puts real fear in me! Fight naturally is way down the list on a horse's menu of options. A horse tends to flee at all costs first. A horse may shut down or attempt to push a person out of the way. But only in quite a serious case will a horse choose to come after a person violently. It does happen. Yet, such aggressive behavior is usually fueled by some pretty horrible previous experiences with humans and/or being backed into a corner. The point, though, is that it is not a typical response for horses to get violent with people.

On the other hand, dogs are hard wired to hunt for a living. Violence is a direct benefit to their livelihood whereas it is not that way for horses. This fact seems to put a dog's willingness to go to aggression and follow through on it way closer to the surface than with horses. And it is my experience with rescue dogs who come from a variety of backgrounds that if dogs signal to you with growling and showing of teeth, you better watch out because they probably mean business.

And I will be the first to admit that I am not a professional at dealing with aggressive behavior in dogs and that it is a very unsettling situation for me when it shows up. Sometimes with rescue dogs, this aggressive reaction to my presence is short lived. The dog is new to me and unsure, and I guess errs on the side of caution, signaling that he will shoot first and ask questions later, as the saying goes. And with a little bit of careful introduction, the teeth disappear, the tail starts wagging, and we become fine friends from then on. I like those instances.

But that is not always the case. I would love to think of myself as a capable dogman who can help support any such dogs to a better place, but I am not handy enough to work through some of the tougher cases at this point.

Some of the dogs that had strong negative reactions to me and other people initially went on to become fine dogs for folks. They let go of the threatening behavior once they learned that people can be okay and/or had special help from capable professional trainers. With these dogs, having a bunch of loving volunteers working with them helped produce excellent results and a change of thinking for the better.

Sometimes dogs have aggressive behavior managed by going into very specific circumstances. For example, living with a single person who never takes the dog anywhere outside of his own yard and is never around children. Thus a very controlled environment at times is used to help support some tough dogs to feel safe and act okay in homes. This may not really fix the problem but it is one way some difficult dogs manage to have a successful life with people. Still others never let go of the aggression and perplex the people who make serious efforts to get a positive change in their behavior. Sometimes these dogs get sent to professional trainers for help with success, but that is not always a cure.

Overall, I see aggression in dogs that is backed by a willingness to see it through way more than I do in horses. And the pack dynamic probably fosters some of this. Dogs and horses both will turn on one another. But with horses I see mainly posturing and then things get settled and life goes on with the order of things sorted out. Since we humans are making the decisions of which horses get put together and in the physical spaces where horses must live, horses are not able to make those choices for themselves and it causes or adds to problems occurring and violence breaking out between horses or towards people and other horses. And clearly stallions will fight one another, but that is a very specific circumstance related to breeding and bands of mares, etc. Dogs, on the other hand, I have seen be really dog aggressive, and in a way that they hold onto as horses do not. Dogs, too, are in unnatural human controlled environments. But, there is no doubt in my mind that in general dogs keep aggression with their own kind and people on the menu of options much more readily than do horses. And that is a serious reality that I keep much more at the forefront of my mind when working with dogs.

Even Ellie Mae, who I think of as a real sweetheart, had an aggressive streak when she got into a situation where she felt vulnerable. Trying to rub her belly was a big one—she did not like that, and honestly, there were few times in her life that I could get that done with her letting down. When going to the vet, if the vet techs were taking her back for some reason away from me, I would suggest that they consider muzzling her. I offered this advice for the very fact that normal interactions with Ellie Mae would never lead one to think that she might turn aggressive. But in the right situation she would start to go there. She would defend herself with a good offense and seriously consider snapping at a person.

I would have loved to defuse that behavior...I should say that I would love to have gotten Ellie Mae to let go of the thinking that she needed to defend herself, but it never did clear out.

It did improve over time, and I worked on it from many angles, like intervening with a correction when it came up and getting super lovey-dovey in general and trying to overwhelm it with good vibes, but ultimately it was in there deep and I never got it cleared out like I wanted to.

Another way to explain her situation was with doing tricks, and this had more to do with other dogs than people, really. I had Ellie Mae performing a really decent roll over. If we were alone in the yard, or even if I was showing off to another person outside, Ellie Mae would perform a really nice roll over. But if any dog, including Carol's large Giant Schnauzer/Bull-mastiff mix Zeke was around, who was a good buddy to her, she would flatly refuse to roll over and get a bit growly. And I never did get that cleared out.

I wonder to what extent such traits are learned behaviors in dogs and how much they enter the world with them? If something is deep seated in the DNA, good luck altering that mindset. I wonder if dogs just have a certain amount of confidence and that's just all that we have to work with? Or, if confidence can be bolstered by training. It seems that from my discussions with herding dog and police/rescue dog folks that confidence is a trait that they look for right away in picking dogs for those professions. At the very least, the job of training a dog who is naturally confident is made way easier for jobs that require steadfastness and a focused mind.

I ended up with Ellie Mae because she flunked the puppy test for being a police/rescue dog, and her litter had been bred for that purpose. At first, I wondered if that was too early to be making such calls? But the way that she fell apart when she felt vulnerable over time had me thinking that it was a good call not to have put her into a job where confidence is critical for success. And even if the training might have overcome it (and I doubt it would have cleared this out with her) it would have taken a lot more work than with a genuinely more confident dog.

And yet, she was a great dog for me. I never needed her to go bite a criminal or sift through a bomb blasted building for injured people. So our homestead and the life she led here was a very appropriate one for her. Finding those good fits goes a long way to having both happy dogs and happy people. But again, I think how she turned growly and snappy when even a little vulnerability crept into a situation is a good example of how close to the surface a dog's aggression lives, especially compared to a horse.

Chapter Sixteen

So They're Started, So They Go

Another classic and poignant saying of Harry's about horses is, "So they're started, so they go."

It certainly is true with horses!

Over and over again I see horses presenting with issues that derive from early experiences with humans. Such formative interactions can stay solidly with horses for their lifetimes, for better or for worse. And the thing about it is, if people can cause an issue by how horses are handled early on, then we know that such problems are avoidable by not doing those things in the first place. The trick becomes figuring out what to do and what not to do.

Horses typically enter the world with a healthy helping of curiosity. This is a huge asset to people. We can use horses' inquisitiveness to great benefit when setting up a search in training them. As discussed a bunch in this book already, getting horses' minds present with a person is essential for getting positive work accomplished with them. If a horse is curious, then the horse's mind already may be showing interest to focus on a person.

People, however, have a tendency to just go and make horses do things. People push and pull foals around, drive horses to move, and so on to the point that before long, not only is a horse's curiosity about people gone, but the horse can be con-

Harry has taught one colt starting clinic over the years, and the two-week event in 2014 was the basis for my trilogy, Six Colts, Two Weeks. "So they're started, so they go," was an oft quoted refrain during that clinic. Here, Harry rides his saddle horse Easy and works Smoke, one of the youngsters, with a flag showing how one can build softness and relaxation into many early experiences between horses and people.

vinced that people are not a good deal. If people handle things poorly, horses can learn pretty quickly to tense up and evade us humans the moment we show up to work with them. But handled well, we can set up searches in our interactions with horses right from the start so that foals begin to figure out what works well and feels good between us. This kind of approach works to produce a willing horse partner who wants to be with a person and trusts a person, and I think this also is true with dogs.

I need only mention the rescue dogs I have seen that were messed up due to previously abusive situations to prove this point. Cowering dogs like Kona, mentioned earlier, tend not to get to a state of horrible worry and ill feelings about humans on their own. People prove to them over and over again that there is a good reason to be worried about us humans. But Kona, as bad off as she was, also showed that positive change is possible.

And people certainly make dogs do things, often by default. They drag them on leashes. If small enough, people just pick dogs up and put them places rather than getting the dogs' minds present and on board with what is being asked. People sometimes punish dogs for not performing what the person thinks that they should. These critters might be happy to go along with human requests willingly if things were made clear and set up right from early on in the training.

But shifting a horse's or dog's negative perception of people once it is established is not always easy or even completely possible, from what I have witnessed. It is by far better to set things up in a positive way from the beginning. And to do this, we humans need to prepare ourselves in the best possible way we can to establish the kind of relationships that produce happy, relaxed, and willing partners in our dogs. It is up to us with our big human brains to do what we can to understand how to train horses and dogs from the beginning. It may be a bit dizzying trying to find good help in this department for a beginner—after all, if you are not sure what is good or bad advice, how do you decide who to go with and what to believe? There are, however, mountains of information and trainers out there to get researching to help get started on one's own dogmanship improvement.

This topic brings me to another stark difference to consider between canines and equines. Horses are born hitting the ground being fully functional horses. Within minutes, a newborn foal is up, taking in the world, and trotting along beside its mother. Dogs, on the other hand, are born helpless little fluff balls that can't even see for many days. In both cases, people can have a tendency to treat the foals and puppies very differently from their adult counterparts, but this can be the very reason some of the more undesirable behaviors get started.

It is fairly easy for a person to push a foal around. Once that creature is 200, 400, and 1200 pounds, pushing a horse around becomes a lot more difficult, and guess who might start doing the pushing? If the horse's mind doesn't understand real benefits from following what the much smaller human presents, good luck on the human making the adult horse do things. This is one spot where so many people end up frustrated.

Right from the first minute of a foal's life, if people treat a foal like they would any older horse (getting the mind present, working to get the horse following a feel, etc.) then a positive relationship can be started that is based on getting a willingness from the horse and building in a good feel with humans. A foal is inexperienced in worldly things, so we may need to give lots of time for them in the beginning to search out answers with us. But still, a foal is a horse and the process of getting a foal's mind focused and with us is the same as it is with a more mature horse.

Similarly, puppies are devastatingly cute. This can lead to people doing all kinds of counter productive anti-training with them. We humans cuddle and coddle the little furry guys. Then over time, we neglect to get them following what we present and wonder why our growing juvenile dog is becoming a delinquent? We've allowed the dog to completely run amuck because he or she was way too cute to set boundaries. Of course, a fluff ball who can not see is pretty hard to start training, but very soon with puppies, as Jack says, getting them to know their names and be able to take corrections is really important. Otherwise, a puppy is learning to boss around or ignore the human. Once that backwards understanding gets established as the foundation of the relationship with people, the person has a big problem to undo.

The situation mentioned in an earlier chapter about revving up a dog fits here. Humans have a tendency to get all squeaky-voiced and get puppies overly excited. We seem to equate that with happiness in dogs. But is overly exciting the canine mind really a good feeling to dogs? Or is it akin to having an over-the-top child going wild? And just like with foals, one needs to ask the question: once puppies get bigger, are the habits we have put in them or allowed to build in them really the kind of behavior and relationship that we desire with them long term? The time to think about this is before we put that kind of thing into a dog.

But on the positive side of this, we have a tremendous opportunity to help direct a dog towards a healthy and balanced relationship with us humans. I am putting a lot of time and effort into trying to understand and visualize what I need to do—and not do—from the first moments I spend with young dogs to get the healthiest minds and most willing partners. And, as can be seen in previous chapters, this same idea can fit with our introductions to older dogs who are new to a person. As with Titus and Gladys, setting up how the relationship is going to work from the first introductions and being consistent with that can have a dog working well for you even if they revert to other behaviors when with other people.

Working on this really amounts to training the human. That, in turn, helps us help dogs to develop the best possible relationship with people. And re-training ourselves out of old habits can be pretty tough. People can have quite emotional responses when working on improving their horsemanship for this same reason. We necessarily see things in ourselves that must change to get changes in our horses or dogs, and sometimes that requires admitting that we have some of our own junk to get past. But once on the other side of such obstacles, the kind of togetherness and willingness that a dog can show in a relationship to a human is incredibly profound, and worth all of the effort.

Chapter Seventeen

Discipline vs. Punishment

As I now suffer through the long string of months still pining for Ellie Mae and searching for the right young Border Collie to bring home, I have tried reading a few dog books to soothe my tortured soul. To be honest, I've not had great luck. A couple of memoirs involving a fella getting to know Border Collies with good reviews came into my possession last winter. I really did not like them. In fact, I couldn't even get half way through them. I also tried to read a few dog training books this spring, but they likewise didn't appeal to me.

Every year for the past 17 years we have hosted Harry Whitney and Ronnie Moyer for Bible/horsemanship clinics here in Floyd County, Virginia as a fundraiser for Ronnie's ministry. Harry and I often discuss dogs, and this year at the clinic one evening Harry recollected a couple of books to me that he had enjoyed some years ago: *Lessons from a Sheep Dog* and *A Shepherd Looks at Psalm 23*. Both books are by Phillip Keller, and one involved a Border Collie. Once the clinics wrapped up, I wasted no time finding used copies online and ordering them.

The books arrived the other day and I began reading *Lessons from a Sheep Dog*. Right in the beginning I came across a passage that got me thinking more about a topic that has grabbed my attention with horses for a long time: discipline. Discipline has become a bit of a dirty word in our culture in recent years. The connotation seems now to be equated with punishment or even abuse, but that is not the meaning of discipline. A disciple is one who follows, and discipline means simply to teach one to follow.

The result of discipline is that one learns to submit to another. Aha! There's another word that likewise has taken on a negative connotation in our culture: submission. Submission is a voluntary giving up of one's will to follow another. Why does this need to be viewed strictly in a negative way? Tyranny is not inherent in submission. How would it look if a child did not submit to a caring parent who instructs that running into a busy street is not a good idea?

Lessons from a Sheep Dog is autobiographical and in it Keller discusses a very problematic Border Collie called Lass. The dog came to him from being chained up in a suburban setting, a far cry from a farm or ranch setting that would allow the Border Collie's natural instincts and drive to be put to proper use. Keller hopes that Lass can be transformed into being the kind of dog that she was bred to be and can help him work the sheep on his new ranch. As things began to shape up in some ways, there were times where Lass lost the plot. These behaviors, "only wasted her energies, sapped her strength, and caused her to break faith," Keller observed.

Keller continues, "She would have to be corrected for her failure to be faithful in the line of duty.

"These were difficult moments for the both of us. But they were absolutely essential for her wellbeing and mine. The operation of the ranch and our success depended in large measure upon her implicit obedience."

The corrections/discipline that Heller mentions that he applied amounted to Lass's sensing that he was disappointed in her. "She knew at once when a coolness came between us," he explains.

And once the discipline was over, Heller held the dog and caressed her and, "her eye would shine again. There was total reconciliation, restoration. In pure pleasure she would leap from my arms, race around the grass in a wide circle, and come leaping back into my warm embrace."

As I read this passage, I once again began to ponder the difference between discipline and punishment, and how that looks in practice in the human/dog and human/horse relationships. And what are the outcomes that both produce?

We've covered that discipline is teaching one to follow, so what exactly is punishment? Punishment can be defined as the infliction of some kind of painful circumstance for a misdeed. So that begs the question, is a correction to a dog punishment? I would say no. But the two things do resemble one another. In fact, to confuse things even more, handled one way an action may be a correction and handled another way the same action may be a punishment.

To begin considering the difference between the two, right away my mind went to thinking about timing. In both horses and dogs, once the moment where an action takes place is over, neither of these creatures is able to return to it in their understanding as humans are able to do. This is true for both positive and negative situations—indeed, any situation. So, for instance, if a treat trainer wanted to give a treat to reward an action a dog did five minutes ago, that is to no avail. The dog never will relate that belated treat to the former action. The dog is now in this moment, and whatever happens now will be linked to the treat that is given now.

Likewise, correcting a dog for some previous undesirable action is fruitless. If the dog got your steak off of the counter five minutes ago and you walk in to find your main course gone and then correct your dog for the missing steak, the dog will have no idea why you are acting in a crazy way. The dog can not make the link back to taking the steak in the past. And a really big rub to bear in mind is, if a human reprimands a dog for something that happened earlier than now, the dog is likely to just become dubious of the person. The "negative" treatment of the dog combined with confusion about why it is taking place interferes with the dog's perceptions of trustworthiness and stability in the human and thereby works against building a positive and willing relationship with a dog. An ill timed correction thus, it seems, falls into the punishment category.

This goes back to anthropomorphizing—giving animals human traits that they do not possess. People are able to understand why today they finally got caught by the police for stealing something two months ago. The jail time they endure for their past deeds is a perfectly clear consequence to them. Likewise, on the positive end of things, the medical degree a doctor spends years attaining is clearly understood to have been the precursor to a mighty fine surgical career. Dogs and horses do not have the mindset to connect the dots on those kinds of causes and effects in their lives. They live in the moment.

The fact that they can learn and adapt in some ways still does not indicate this kind of human thinking. Rather, it just shows that dogs and horses can identify tendencies (what is a threat to them and should be avoided, what is a comfort to them and draws them, etc.) but they do not link specific memories to current actions as humans can. So, they are perfectly capable of learning, for instance, that passing people when on leash doesn't work out as well as following people does—if the corrections presented by people are done as the dog is in the process of passing them. But make that correction even a matter of seconds too late and the dog likely will not relate that correction to what took place just previously.

A well timed correction made with a dog at the very time of a problem is easy for a dog to relate to what is taking place. If you catch the dog with his nose on the counter right at your rib eye and make a correction right then, then the dog will know for certain that putting his nose on the counter with food near does not work out well. Also, if we are able to make our correction timely, there is an opportunity to redirect the dog. Not only do we discourage the undesirable behavior, but we also can offer an alternative desired behavior to the dog that then sets that up to work out well.

Recently when I was discussing discipline versus punishment with Harry, he brought up a really good point. Harry posed a question as an answer: "are we doing it to them or for them?" This query presents a simple yet profound way to think about this.

Punishment has a feel to it, and Harry's statement really captures that idea. Punishing a dog, for example, often is accompanied by anger from the human. The person, in actual fact, desires to inflict pain on the dog because the person feels that the dog deserves to suffer for the crime committed. Discipline, however, is undertaken for the very benefit of the dog—to produce understanding and get the dog to follow the person's ideas more willingly. This makes me think about Keller who points out more than once how it deeply hurt him to discipline Lass but he loved her too much to leave her a wreck with a very questionable future. Discipline, if successful, might allow Lass to become a help to the ranch instead of a hazard who would have to go.

Let's stick with a sheep dog for an example. If the dog has a wild streak and wants to attack the sheep he is supposed to help care for, that is a terrible liability and can not be tolerated by a rancher. So if the dog's wellbeing is to be preserved, there must be a change of mind that leads to a change of heart that leads to a change of behavior in the dog. And a handler may need to get pretty big in some way to get a change of mind in a dog who wants to attack a sheep. But if the getting big is being done for the benefit of the dog, then it will have a very different feel, timing, and outcome to it than if a dog is getting punished and the person's actions are simply being done to the dog as a personal retribution.

Similarly, a pet dog who wants to chase cars is in extreme danger of being injured or killed. If discipline can be implemented to change the mindset that causes the dog to chase cars, then that discipline has been done for the dog and is not punishment.

With horses, I learned from Harry long ago that it is important to get big enough to get a horse's attention and get a change. But, to try and dial that in to be just big enough without going overboard. Getting too big can overwhelm the horse and create more worry and tension, and the horse can become troubled about the person. To make this really tricky, what is big enough for one horse to make a nice change may be nowhere near big enough for a less sensitive horse. I have found this to be true with dogs, too.

The range of rescue dogs that I have worked with have been all over the place in this regard. Sometimes a worried, sensitive dog needs only the slightest sound or look from me to start paying attention and fall in line with what I am offering. At other times, a boisterous, ping-pong brained dog may need a pretty big correction to get his mind centered up and hear what is being offered. But again, even with the more difficult dogs who require getting bigger corrections to make changes, how corrections are presented has everything to do with how they are perceived. Are they perceived as punishments done to them, that can create a road block between the person and the dog? Or are corrections taken as discipline, done for them so that they are able to find a better spot with the person?

With dogs, I have been able to get big at times, as with Titus, and had dogs fall in line pleasantly with me on the leash. I've also been challenged and not had a dog be quite so capable of grasping what I am trying to say. But generally, it is my experience that good discipline is worth all the effort of figuring out how to get it working. The relationship with a happy dog who willingly follows what you offer (submits) is profoundly enjoyable, apparently to both parties.

Chapter Eighteen
My Next Dog

My fascination with Border Collies goes back at least a decade. For nearly that long I have known that my next dog is going to be a Border Collie. I decided not to get another dog until after Ellie Mae had finished out her days with me. That sad, inevitable moment came late last year when she presented with lymphoma. So now, I pine for a dog to call my own and the Border Collie search is on in earnest.

I am not quite sure how the Border Collie breed got on my radar. Probably it was a combination of seeing some Border Collies owned by horse people that I met around the country and hearing many stories about their intelligence and abilities. Also, having grown up on a large dairy farm, I spent plenty of my youth herding and handling Holsteins. So working stock seems to position some puzzle piece into place inside me, and I enjoy it.

Only a bit later in life when I began to be exposed to beef cattle, cow horses, and cow dogs did I put two and two together and ask the obvious question: why didn't we use horses and/or dogs to help with our cow tasks on the farm? Twice a day every day we herded over a hundred milk cows out of a large pasture into the pens to go into the milking parlor. Not to mention all of the other heifer, milk cow, sick cow, and dry cow shuffling that often went on.

Many years ago now when I was writing for a ton of major horse magazines, I decided to try and find someone using horses to move dairy cattle. I searched and searched in many different ways, and I came up with none—not a single one anywhere in the country. So, I decided to explore why there was such an absence of equine help on dairy farms.

Perhaps it is not surprising that the one person in the world I found with at least an insight into this mystery was Baxter Black. Baxter was a veterinarian and commentator known for his rural wit and wisdom and spent two decades sharing it on NPR radio, in more than 30 books, in magazines, on TV, and finally (once it was invented) on the Internet.

So I called Baxter and explained the difficulty I was having finding any dairy farmers who used horses to work their cattle even though it seemed like a perfectly logical fit.

Baxter said something like, "Well, Tom, it's pretty simple."

I was all ears. But rather than tell me about someone who was using a horse to move dairy cattle, he explained to me why I never would find one. Baxter clarified that there are ranchers and there are farmers. Ranchers will do anything they can not to get down out of the saddle while working. Farmers, by contrast, will avoid using horses for work at all costs.

Baxter then cracked me up further by saying that a farmer will use a truck, a tractor, a four-wheeler, a backhoe, a riding lawnmower, and even a bicycle to move cows to avoid using a horse. That this clear and distinct mindset is sacred and, as far as he knew, never violated.

And apparently, it is true.

Dairy farmers may be solidly against equines being on the payroll, but Baxter still did not illuminate me on the real underlying reasons why this is. I wonder if perhaps it has to do with the conversion of farmers from using draft animals to tractors for farm work? Perhaps whatever psychological and economic shifts that occurred for that to take place also created a deep seated machinery culture to get more work done with less manure?

I do know from experience that dairy farmers are not against dogs. But here again, they seem to resist the kind of dog that could be a real help to them the most—that is, a herding dog with an outrun. A Border Collie or Kelpie would love nothing more than to head out into a pasture and/or woods, steep or flat, and bring in the cows. With a little finesse, the dog even could cut cows out of the herd, a job I constantly was doing afoot when growing up for all kinds of reasons.

On the farm where I grew up, for example, there were Dobermans. Yes, Dobermans. Great for deterring dubious looking potential thugs (of which there were few on a 1,000 acre farm in the middle of nowhere in rural Virginia), but not so helpful when it came to moving cattle. Well, maybe I should restate that...not so helpful when moving cattle in the particular direction that one wants them to go. Beautiful dogs, though, and not bad truck dogs, to tell you the truth. There was one who liked to chase flying buzzards at various distances. He'd even see one flying way up, miles away and off he'd go running across the fields barking after it. Not really helpful or particularly understandable, but, you know, whatever—he eventually came back and obviously never caught one.

Many years ago now I penned an article for *Eclectic Horseman* magazine on working stock with dogs while the person is horseback. It began:

A capable hand partnered with a good horse and a well trained stock dog is held in very high esteem across the ranchlands of America. So much so, in fact, that such a trio often is reputed to be as effective as a posse of dogless cowboys ahorseback when it comes to working stock.

The idea came from my own desire to learn more about this kind of work and talk to people who know about it. I remember a light bulb moment when I was talking to Bryan Neubert. Bryan is a horsemanship clinician and cowboy who has managed some pretty large ranches and worked a lot with horses, dogs, cattle, and cowboys over the years.

Bryan explained how one good cow dog is extremely valuable to a cowboy. Some of these top end, well trained dogs even can sell for five figures. Bryan explained that from a business perspective, you pay once for the dog and then you don't have to pay him a salary over time. Also, there's no insurance to pay, the dog doesn't get disgruntled or call in to take days off, and a good dog quite literally can do the work of two or more cowboys. Plus, the dog can get into thickets and other spots where a person on a horse can't go. It becomes quite easy to see what an amazing help and excellent investment a good working dog can be on a ranch or farm.

Also for the above mentioned article, I interviewed Mindy Bower. Mindy starts horses and teaches horsemanship from her Uh-Oh ranch in Kiowa, Colorado. Mindy has decades of experience working with herding dogs from horseback. This part of my interview with Mindy often comes to mind when I think about Border Collies and horses working together:

Aside from training a herding dog to work stock while she's horseback, Mindy's experience has taught her that using a seasoned stock dog in tandem with stock also can be a very helpful tool for training the stock horse, too.

"If you have a horse that's a little bit worried about stock," Mindy explains, "it's really nice to use sheep because sheep are real easy to manage if you have a good dog. You can go out into the pasture with the sheep, and the horse might be having a heart attack, so you just bring your dog around in between you and the sheep and start to push the sheep away from you. Once the sheep are starting to move, you can get the horse to follow the sheep.

"And then, if the horse starts to get more comfortable, you could send the dog around to stop the sheep. As time goes by, you can get the dog to bring the sheep towards you. If the horse starts

to get scared again, then you just flank the dog around and push the sheep away from you and really work on the bad spot because you're able to control your dog and you can get the horse confident. Eventually, your dog can bring the sheep right around the horse, and the sheep can go under the horse and around it, and then pretty soon you're standing in the middle of the sheep. That is such a great experience—it's like riding with a school of fish. It's really fun!"

Man, would I ever love to have a dog to do such things with sheep as I work horses! Mindy here has provided even more good ideas for jobs for a dog to do with me. And that image of sheep flowing all around and even under one's saddle horse has been stuck in my head ever since we spoke about it.

So, back to my quest for a new dog. First, having lost Ellie Mae when she was 12 years old not all that long ago, I am dead set against getting an older dog, even though I am happy to consider a rescue. I just can't bring myself to start with, say, a four-year-old who may be a third of the way to the end of his or her lifespan. Getting a dog who is on the brink of beginning the older phase of dog life with clouding eyes and a whitening muzzle is painful to consider. I want to invest a ton of time into my new dog to get things going well and be able to spend a full dog's lifespan with her or him.

Starting with a puppy would give us maximum dog lifetime time together. Puppies are cute, but they are a ton of work. I am fine to go through the puppy stage, though. We just did it with Carol's dog Victor, and the process is both wonderful and frustrating. Part of me is keen to do that as I want this next dog to be the ultimate companion dog and go everywhere with me all the time. Starting from the beginning would provide an opportunity for me to set things up the way I want them to be (assuming I don't screw some things up; a very real possibility). But on the other hand, the personality and abilities of a dog may not be particularly evident at a very young age. Seeing attributes like confidence, intensity, and natural herding instincts may not be completely clear in a young pup. Getting a dog closer to, say, eight months to a year old might be helpful in my quest for finding the ultimate dog for my situation. That might be especially helpful if the dog is a rescue and the dog's parents are unknown. But, one of the benefits of going right to a reputable breeder is that the health and dispositions of the parents and their blood lines can be known with confidence.

So here's what I am thinking. I definitely want a Border Collie. I want a full blooded Border Collie, not a mix, because I have a fascination with the breed and I want to work with one without the influence of other breeds in there. I want to work stock, and I want to experience a dog with an outrun (how Border Collies go out and around and gather stock, and can work the stock back towards the handler).

Realistically, though, getting to work stock with my dog will not be a daily or weekly occurrence. Going to feed horses, fix fence, haul hay, riding in the truck to give horse lessons, being in the office here hopefully chilling while I work on some writing...that's more along the lines of what life is like for a dog with me. I am looking for a dog capable of being with me in all of these varied situations in a mindful manner. A super intense working bred Border Collie may be suitable in this situation if the dog also is able to let that drive go and be mentally with me when I ask. But then again, I wonder if there may be Border Collies who are genetically so intense for herding that to get some companion/pet time with them daily might be working against their nature and that it may be a real chore to get them sober minded?

I love having jobs for my dog, and training tricks, and expecting the dog to be a real companion. Getting some of that working clearly is in the training and handling. I sure hope that I can bring one along who can be sober of mind, willing when working, and happy to be both with me or on his or her own if I need to leave the dog in the house or the truck while I do something. I do hope to find a Border Collie with breeding that does not work against such a lifestyle.

From talking with others who have Border Collies in that kind of daily life situation, I find that the breed can do very well, so I am encouraged. The gal who cuts my hair has one. Ty hangs out going in and out of the house at will as people come and go getting haircuts. He does very well and seems especially to like kids, although he remains a bit aloof and is not the kind

Ellie Mae, now able to sit relaxed at a distance from me when I ask her to from atop Niji. (Photo: Carol Moates)

of dog who wants a bunch of petting and cuddling. He loves to play with his toys, and yet will curl up and seems happy to keep on eye on all of the activity, as well. Ty has learned to open and close the storm door to outside, so he can come and go as he pleases during the day.

I know of several people who have Border Collies who tag along with them in the house, on the farm, hopping into trucks, cars, or four-wheelers to accompany the human on daily chores and tasks. We'll see how it works out for me, and that'll no doubt provide plenty of material for another book. You can bet I'll be keeping notes as I see how my life with a Border Collie progresses!

End Note

Wrapping up this book is a tough one. On the one paw, I have a strong sense that I am not finished with what needs to be said. But if my horsemanship experience and writings are any insight into this impression, the feeling of not having said it all will be the case no matter how thick this book becomes.

On another paw, that is true because I know I have so much more to learn about how dogs operate and how humans can approach them to get the best, most willing, and happy relationships.

On yet another paw, as much knowledge, experience, and capabilities in relationship building as I can claim with horses, I am light years away from exhausting what can be known about bettering humans' relationships with horses, let alone dogs.

And on the final paw, many of the ruminations shared in this book have banged around in my head for long enough that I am exceedingly glad now to have at least this much put down on the page. The act of writing it down allows me to see more clearly if what I have been thinking makes sense. Adding some new thoughts and connections to what I already have been kicking around also has been helpful in my own quest to get better with dogs.

Perhaps there are as many questions brought to light by this book as answers. But, even the questions point in a foundational way to the potential in horses and dogs for profoundly deep kinds of connections with people that are beneficial to both species. And, that it is up to us humans—indeed, it is our responsibility if we choose to own these marvelous creatures—to do all that we can to figure out how to best unlock that potential, especially for the benefit of the animals in our care.

Particular details about what one should or shouldn't do with a dog can be debated on and on. But it is safe to say that developing a relationship that reduces a dog's stress is a positive endeavor and worthy of investment. Also, having a dog who is pleased to follow and can understand and willingly undertake what an owner asks is a positive quality, and makes for a happy life.

At this moment, I sit in Utah having just wrapped up teaching a very fun horsemanship clinic. There were a pack of dogs that lived on the farm where the clinic was held—a sprawling place with at least hundred head of horses between the boarders and the owners' breeding stock. There were Border Collie crosses and one Kelpie cross. And as boarders came and went doing their horse things, I saw other dogs with those humans, too, including one gorgeous Border Collie.

That horse person went about her chores with the Border Collie on a leash keeping the dog close to her. I wondered if the dog was new to her? It looked like a grown dog, so what I observed was unlikely to be a particularly early stage of training. I, too, expect to go about horse chores with my new Border Collie tethered to me. I noticed at one point that the dog was able to lie down quietly by the person's car with the leash dropped to the ground and remain there contentedly as the person entered a pasture full of horses to tend to her horse. And my thought drifted forward to the future when I might be working on that at home.

I fully expect the next phase of being a dog owner to be a very interesting one. I hope that my horsemanship will make me a better dogman. I know that my time spent with Ellie Mae and my successes and failures with her will better my ability to set things up with the new pup. I also hope that my ponderings put down here will resonate with others and maybe kick up a few ideas that might prove helpful and fun for you readers, as well.

So now, off to find my next dog and see if I am trainable. Am I catching on to what's really important. Will I be able to get the depth of relationship and willingness that I hope for? Will we be able to work some stock together, this new Border Collie and me?

Who knows, but it sure sounds like there's a book in there somewhere....

A couple of all-time, truly great dogs—Bootsy, our son Shiloh's Pit Bull on the left and Teeney Weeney, Carol's Rhodesian Ridegeback/English Mastiff cross on the right tagging along with us checking horses.

About the Author

Tom Moates is an award winning writer on the masthead of *Equus* magazine and his articles have run in many magazines including: *Eclectic Horseman*, *America's Horse*, and *Western Horseman*. Moates's previous books include the *Six Colts, Two Weeks* trilogy, *Discovering Natural Horsemanship, A Horse's Thought, Between the Reins, Further Along the Trail, Going Somewhere, Passing It On*, *Round-Up: A Gathering of Equine Writings, Mane Thoughts,* and *Considering Horsemanship*. Moates also recently took a foray into fiction with *The Old Sleeper*, a spy novel.

Moates lives on a solar powered homestead with his wife Carol, a pack of dogs, and a herd of horses in the Blue Ridge Mountains of Virginia. Book ordering info, horsemanship clinic and lesson info, and Moates's latest publishing news are available at www.TomMoates.com.

Ellie Mae.

www.ingramcontent.com/pod-product-compliance
Ingram Content Group UK Ltd.
Pitfield, Milton Keynes, MK11 3LW, UK
UKHW041823200726
13854UKWH00002BA/532